L 8950

THE HAPPIEST DAYS

Staircase to the Upper School, Eton

G. F. LAMB

The Happiest Days

London
MICHAEL JOSEPH

First published by
MICHAEL JOSEPH LTD
26 Bloomsbury Street,
*London, W.C.*1
1959

© *copyright* 1959 *by G. F. Lamb*

Set and printed in Great Britain by Tonbridge Printers Ltd, Peach
Hall Works, Tonbridge, Kent, in Bembo twelve on thirteen point, on
paper made by Henry Bruce at Currie, Midlothian, and bound by
James Burn at Esher, Surrey

CONTENTS

ILLUSTRATIONS

PREFACE

There are many aspects of education. In this sketch of school life during the last three or four centuries I have chosen to stress the more colourful features. Probably the main characteristic of most people's schooldays in this century is a mild tedium; but tedium is no more interesting to read about then it is to endure. It is the highlights that attract our attention. Paradoxically, the highlights in education have most often been dark. I must, however, warn the reader that the picture has not been falsified. Most of the details come from authentic autobiographical records and standard histories.

It happens that I do not care much for class distinctions in education and that I believe the merits of boarding-schools are often overrated. But this book is by no means intended as an attack upon the so-called public schools; and I have chosen my material mainly from these schools, simply because this type of education has been very much more fully and more vividly documented than any other. There is almost a library of books on Eton College alone.

By and large, the modern day grammar school probably offers to pupils of the requisite ability the most satisfactory education obtainable at any kind of school (for which reason one must deplore the threats made against it on political grounds in favour of unwieldy Comprehensive monsters). But I hope no reader will be so foolish as to suppose that because a great deal was wrong with education in the past, everything must therefore be right with education today. Schooling is a reflection of the age in which it takes place. We have to some extent cured the individual brutalities and the staff laxity in supervision which too often shamed the schools of the eighteenth and nineteenth centuries; but our modern schools too often reflect the laxity in discipline and the ugly gang spirit, cinema-fostered, which are characteristic of our day and age. In recent weeks we have seen gang warfare on a large scale between the pupils of two large secondary modern schools in the south because a boy at one school went out one evening with a girl friend of a boy at the other; and we have seen a new master at a secondary modern school in the north attacked and hustled in a public street by a mob of two hundred boys because he had threatened to punish one of them for bad behaviour.

It is probably true that potential writers and artists, being more sensitive than most of their fellows, have often (though by no means always) experienced more suffering at school, and have subsequently been more articulate about their experiences. This is a point to be remembered; but it still does not invalidate their records. An unpleasant experience is no less real because it is exceptional. Nor are all the unpleasant experiences as exceptional as we may like to believe. Many of the testifiers have been budding scientists, men of action, or just ordinary chaps; and even the creative writers have sometimes spoken for Everyman and not just for themselves.

When all is said, however, the book is far from being merely a Chamber of Horrors. Fun and Games, as well as Fagging and Flogging, find a place in it. In accumulating material I constantly asked myself two significant questions. The first was, 'Is it interesting?' The second was, 'Is it true?' If the answer to both questions was an affirmative, then I gathered the fruit and dropped it in my basket.

In a book of this kind one has to adopt a policy as regards footnotes. It is a book for the general reader, and to give a source reference for every statement of fact or quotation would turn it into an academic thesis. Even to allow the reference notes to lurk at the back of the book (with little numerals dotted about the pages of each chapter) can be disturbing to someone who is reading for pleasure. I have therefore avoided giving sources except where the information seemed specifically desirable. But all the material here gathered together is to be found in the books or journals listed in the Bibliography, and he who runs to the London Library or the British Museum may read it.

THE BEST SCHOOL OF ALL

> They were great days and jolly days
> At the best school of all.
>
> SIR HENRY NEWBOLT

> O the great days, in the distance enchanted,
> Days of fresh air, in the rain and the sun.
>
> EDWARD E. BOWEN

> The blackest and most odious period of my existence arrived—I was sent to St Paul's School.
>
> MR SERJEANT BALLANTINE

> Personally I hated school . . . I hated the bell which drove us up in the mornings; I hated the masters; I hated being whacked; above all I hated the work.
>
> SIR PATRICK HASTINGS

> My whole time at Wellington was so disgusting and useless that I find myself hardly able to write about it without nausea.
>
> LORD GRANTLEY

> Twelve years ago I was a boy
> A happy boy at Drury's.[1]
>
> W. M. PRAED

> I liked Eton, except in the following respects: for work and games, for boys and masters.
>
> SIR OSBERT SITWELL

1 A boarding-house at Eton

Oh when I was a tiny boy
My days and nights were full of joy
    My mates were blithe and kind!
No wonder that I sometimes sigh,
And dash the teardrop from my eye
    To cast a look behind.

THOMAS HOOD
(Clapham Academy)

How I did loathe that preparatory school—preparatory, thank heaven, for a life that was not to be. Mine has not been a dull one or an unhappy one after all.

HERMAN MERIVALE

Though my way of life has made me acquainted with all sorts of men, from the highest to the lowest, I deliberately affirm that the society I fell into at school was the worst I have ever known.

T. H. HUXLEY

Never merrier song and laughter,
    Never the voice of truer joy,
Have you heard ere now, or shall hear hereafter,
    Than rings from the lips of the Marlborough
                                    boy.

C. L. F. BOUGHEY

The knoutings I received from my reverend master's arm turned my back all the colours of the rainbow; and when I screamed from the fearful torture they produced, the headmaster sent a prefect down to say if I made such a horrid noise he also would have a go at me.

EDWARD LOCKWOOD
(Marlborough)

CHAPTER ONE

SHINING MORNING FACE

READINESS to offer a friendly welcome to strangers is one of the marks of a civilised community. The traditional welcome to new boys at school has long been to punch their heads, jeer at them, or, at the best, ignore them altogether.

In earlier days the treatment was usually a good deal rougher than this. At Winchester in the eighteen-forties, for example, a favourite trick was to ask the greenhorn if he possessed a pair of tin gloves. When a negative reply was received—and it invariably was—the older boy would kindly undertake to provide a pair; which he did by snatching a blazing stick from the Chamber fire, blowing out the flame, and drawing the red-hot end up the back of the youngster's hand from each knuckle to the wrist, and then two or three lines at right angles, leaving the skin a mass of blisters. He would then ask the new boy if he was of Founder's Kin, and, whatever the answer, test it by trying to break a plate over his head, the theory being that if the plate broke before the head, the descent from the founder of the College was proved.

Blundell's School, at about the same period, carried this type of welcome a stage further. Big boys would strap a new boy face downward to a portable bench and place him with his back close to the big fire. To prevent him from actually scorching they would baste him from time to time with cold water. If he was hardy enough to survive this treatment without showing signs of fear, then he would be accepted as one of the school. If he wilted or showed fear or resisted, then he would be marked out for further bullying.

The story goes that on one occasion some excitement drew

the boys from the basting process to the Green outside. When they returned, the victim was so badly burned as to be beyond aid, and died soon afterwards. Some smaller boys were present, it is quite plausibly said, but were afraid to help the victim for fear of being put in his place when the older boys returned. One would like to reject this as the sort of episode that occurs in the more melodramatic type of school story, were it not that there are so many indisputable records of actual experience that make the incidents of *Eric* and *St Winifred's* seem rather tame. It is worth noting here that even so fervid a Blundellian as the late F. J. Snell is reluctant to discredit the tale. 'It cannot,' he regrets, 'be dismissed as entirely imaginative.'

There is certainly no dismissing a Marlborough College episode related by Sir Cyril Norwood, who saw the resulting scar seventy years later. In 1850 a new boy, eight years old, was strapped to a bench, in front of a whole crowd of other boys, and branded with a large anchor on the forearm by means of a red-hot poker. As a result he spent his first three weeks at the school in the Sick House; but nothing happened to the wielder of the poker, the reverend masters at Marlborough being blind and deaf out of school hours.

One of the completest stories of new boy misery comes from eighteenth-century Westminster. In 1776 a little boy named Frederick Reynolds arrived at the dame's boarding-house where he was to stay, the mistress of which had assured his mother that she would give him every care and attention.

He entered the boys' common room unobserved. A large group of boys was engaged in allotting parts for a dramatic performance. Reynolds stood for a while listening to the noisy arguments, pleased to feel that his future companions had such interesting occupations and wondering, perhaps, if he would be invited to take part.

Suddenly he was seen. There was a tremendous bellow of 'New boy! New boy!' and the whole mob surged upon him. He was roughly seized and pushed on to a table, where he stood trying to acclimatise himself to this boisterousness.

'Which of us will you fight?' they began to shout.

Reynolds imagined they were joking, and tried to respond in the right spirit. 'Any of you,' he replied smiling.

But Westminster was fond of fisticuffs and did not joke about serious things. 'A little tiger-faced brat' about Reynolds' own size cried eagerly: 'Oh you will, will you?' and dragged off his coat without wasting a moment.

The unfortunate new boy, still hardly realising the kind of company he had fallen into, thought that his manner had somehow offended them, and begged their pardons. They replied with coarse shouts, dragged him off the table and began to strip him. Off came his cape . . . This was the eighteenth century, when even children wore what to us would be fancy dress. But young Frederick was more strikingly dressed than was customary, even in those times. He wore a scarlet jacket, a spangled waistcoat, black silk breeches patiently made by his nurse from silk stockings, and white cotton hose—a delicate, unsophisticated child carefully nurtured in a gentle home.

Here was perfect fodder for a gang of Westminster boys, notorious in those days for their hooliganism, and quite ready to beat up a passer-by in Dean's Yard if he happened to offend them. Jeers and mock applause greeted his appearance. Ink was produced, and most boys in the room found some kind of squirt. The scarlet coat, spangled waistcoat, and white hose became as black as the breeches, his face and hands likewise. When this amusement palled, a blanket was dragged from a bed, and the bewildered child endured the famous ceremony of blanket-tossing—not the discreet three tosses of Tom Brown's experience, but a long-continued succession of ascents and descents between blanket and ceiling. 'After suffering the severe torments of every remaining species of manual wit,' he wrote in his adulthood, 'I was at length permitted to crawl into my bed. There I lay, comforting myself with the assurance that torture had done its worst, till I gradually sobbed myself into a sound sleep.'

But the welcome to Westminster School was not yet complete. 'Scarcely had the deep tones of the Abbey bell, tolling the awful hour of midnight, awakened me, when I was alarmed by the loud screams of several of the younger boys. Starting up in a paroxysm of terror, I saw at the foot of the bed a horrid spectre bearing a large cross on which was written in flaming characters, "THINK ON TO-MORROW." I gazed till, stupefied with fear, I mechanically closed my eyes and hid myself under the bedclothes.' This was not good enough for the tormentor. He dragged the bedclothes aside, forcing the child to look, pointed to the glowing letters, and shook his head solemnly before disappearing, leaving his victim dazed by bewildered horror.

All this was many years before older boys and quite young boys were either separated or supervised. It would be difficult to exaggerate the very real terror which was not seldom inflicted on children fresh from a quiet home by a mixture of horse-play and sadism in the dormitories and schoolrooms. Parents, then as in later times, were stoical in enduring their children's sufferings without flinching.

Few more pitiful letters have been written than the desperate note scribbled home by little Frederick Reynolds on the day after this first disastrous evening.

'*My dear dear Mother,*

If you don't let me come home, I die—I am all over ink, and my fine clothes have been spoilt—I have been tost in a blanket, and seen a ghost.

I remain, my dear dear Mother
Your dutiful and most unhappy son
FREDDY

PS. Remember me to my Father.

He did not come home and he did not die; but the mind can suffer many injuries without actually giving up the ghost.

Quite apart from the deliberate unfriendliness of the natives, going to a new school, especially a boarding school, is likely to be a disturbing and even alarming experience for a normal child.

'A boy's experiences when he first enters Eton,' the captain of the College wrote in the eighteen-eighties, 'are more amusing when viewed from a distance then they are at the moment. The perpetual bustle of a large "House," the echoing through the long passages, together with a certain sense of solitariness, make him feel homesick when he is shut up in his own small room . . . The hasty steps up and down the stairs; the shout now and again of "Lower Boy" which makes the new boy jump; the confused feelings with which he stands with his fellow fags ranged against the wall of his fagmaster's room to await his orders—all are very novel and sometimes alarming. He is,' the captain adds, 'naturally subject to a certain amount of petty tyranny.'

The younger the child the more disturbing the experience is likely to be; and for this reason alone, apart from the greater roughness and the more virulent tyranny, education in the old days offered a more violent shock to the new boy at a public school than perhaps it does today. The age of entry was very young, sometimes very young indeed. In Elizabethan times it was often prescribed by school statutes as six to nine. As late as the early nineteenth century boys quite often entered Harrow, for example, at the age of eight; some were as young as seven or even six-and-a-half; in 1752 Samuel Parr, afterwards an assistant master there, entered the school at the age of five.

Although the age of entry to most public schools was in due course raised to well over double figures (it still remains at nine, however, for Christ's Hospital) the problem was merely passed, to some extent, to the preparatory boarding-school, where the young child, despite smaller numbers and sometimes a more homely atmosphere, still frequently felt himself lost and abandoned. 'There was scarcely any misery in life equal to that of the small boy of nine who left home for his first term at a private school.' Sir Basil Thomson, formerly,

among other positions, Assistant Commissioner of the Metro-
politan Police, is writing specifically of his own experience in
the early 'seventies, but he is the mouthpiece of a multitude
of small boys in many periods. D'Arcy Thompson (afterwards
an admirable schoolmaster) was just over seven when he went
to Christ's Hospital, London, in 1837. He compared the experience to being taken in a wheelbarrow whilst fast asleep and
then suddenly flung out in the middle of a busy market. The
school was 'a kind of noisy, multitudinous, ill-regulated city
. . . I collapsed from a little boy into a dwarf, a pygmy, a
hop-o'-my-thumb, a gnat, a nonentity. Years, entire years,
passed over, leaving me still in bewilderment.'

'Though I was soon happy at Summerfield,' Bernard Darwin
writes of himself as a child of ten or eleven, 'the going there
was agonising. The first parting is so blurred with tears that
I cannot recall it in any detail. I feel as if I must have lost
consciousness from grief. The first clear picture I have is of
myself cast down upon my bed, sobbing and bedraggled,
with the room having grown dark in the gathering dusk.'

Darwin was not one of those anti-social or eccentric children
who cannot fit into a community existence. He was just a
normal child suffering intensely from being unnecessarily
deprived, too early in his life, of the security which his home
gave him. And although the misery passed as the term proceeded, it recurred at the beginning of each new term for
some time to come.

There was no particular reason for his banishment; his
parents were merely treading the path of convention. He had
previously attended the Perse School at Cambridge, his home
town, as a day boy, 'but home was there as a background and
refuge.' Strangely enough it did not occur either to his father
or to Bernard Darwin himself, when he came to write his
autobiography, that that is precisely what a home ought to be.

It was, and doubtless still is, the practice in some public
and private schools to provide the newcomer with a guide

during his first week or two. In Sir Osbert Sitwell's preparatory school he was called a Shepherd. At Winchester he was a one-year fellow known as a *Tege* (pronounced *tee-jay* and derived from the French *protéger*). At Westminster he was a Substance, the new boy being a Shadow. At Charterhouse he was a Father.

There is a comforting sound to the words Shepherd and Father, though the person was often less agreeable than the word. (Not all shepherds love their sheep, as Sitwell discovered.) It is sensible that the customs and traditions of an institution should be personally explained to those who are entering it, and a slightly older boy who has fairly recently become familiar with them himself may be as good a teacher as any. Customs, good and bad, grow up in every community, and it is as well to know them if we are to live in the community. Moreover, a host of difficulties in everyday matters may well arise if the new boy has no one at hand to put him wise. A well-chosen Substance (or What You Will) could be a godsend.

Unfortunately many schools contrived to reduce a wise practice to absurdity. Not content just to encourage the appointed guide to extend a helping hand to his protégé, they forced him to become a crammer, and a crammer of absurdities. Slang words, nicknames, and all the ridiculous habits and conventions which juvenile communities are apt to indulge in, had to be solemnly expounded and anxiously learnt by heart. Winchester, one of the worst schools for this crystallisation of trivialities, actually produced a book of words, and the new boy was examined in these mysteries after a fortnight, and both he and his *Tege* were beaten if he failed. Charterhouse, too, had its 'new bugs' exam' over which the bug was expected (on pain of a beating) to be able to leap at the end of a fortnight; and similarly at not a few other schools of the type.

There is no harm in slang; nicknames are useful and sometimes amusing; customs, even silly ones, are sometimes convenient. But when a school treats these things as serious and important it has already failed in one of its first educational duties, which is to teach a sense of proportion.

Only boys driven in upon themselves, as they are apt to be in the closed community of a boarding-school, could devise the rigid inanities of some of the great public schools. At Winchester, for example, the 'new man'—there are no boys or chaps at Winchester, only men—could not go for a walk with a friend in another 'House.' The new Colleger dared not put the tail of his gown round his waist—a privilege which could only be enjoyed when there were at least thirty 'men' junior to himself; and the tail could not be carried over his arm until he attained prefect-hood. At Harrow, to quote one of its most distinguished House Captains, 'we had all sorts of un-written rules of suppression in that queer life. You must turn up your trousers; must not go out with your umbrella rolled. Your hat must be worn tilted forward; you must not walk more than two abreast till you reached a certain form.' At Rugby the new boy dared not put his hands in his pockets, or walk on a particular side of the road. At Haileybury his hair was not allowed to be visible below the peak of his cap.

Many of these fashions and fatuities are passed down from generation to generation. Others change with a breath of wind.

'At one time,' wrote Gilbert Coleridge in 1912 of his own Eton schooldays in the 'seventies, 'no lower boy would be seen in a greatcoat, either in school or in chapel, however cold the weather might be, and yet he would put it on to watch a football match. Then suddenly, no one knew why, all lower boys appeared in greatcoats, but none would venture to turn up his collar, obedient to the unwritten law that only swells could do such a thing.

'But the most remarkable taboo was established after I left. No small boy dared walk in High Street on the side opposite the Christopher Hotel; he might cross the street to make a purchase, but not walk there; and I remember the horror expressed by a lower boy, whom I visited some years ago,

The New Boy

when I suggested walking back on that side. "I can't tell you why," he said, "but it simply can't be done".'

This sort of thing is apt to spread, both within the school and without. Other schools are apt to ape the fashionable few, especially in the least desirable ways. Thus J. P. Graham, an enthusiastic master and ex-pupil of Uppingham, writing as late as 1932, condemns what he calls a modern and futile innovation—'a foolish inquisition known as a fags' examination' when the wretched new boy had to show a knowledge of 'every master's lodging-place or nickname, or abstruse and idiotic details of no importance, at short notice.' Not all masters remain so level-headed as Graham about it, for one of the dangers of school-teaching is that the pupil is in the end so often the master, bringing his superior in age to see things from his own schoolboy viewpoint. A Charterhouse master, for example, has included, in his book on the school, a solemn chapter on the school's childish slang without a hint that he is aware of its childishness.

The older school stories used to make great play with the initiation ceremonies which new boys had to undergo— above all the dormitory singing by candlelight, with a violently critical audience sitting around on beds. Critics of these stories have pointed out with irony, gusto, or wit that the new boy at a public school was, in fact, never badgered to make a Roman holiday. Newer school stories were written, showing a young hero, his mind stuffed with Talbot Baines Reed and *Tom Brown's Schooldays*, going off to his alma mater ready for his singing ordeal, and being almost deflated by the discovery that far from being called upon for a chorus, he was simply ignored. These newer stories were regarded as representing realism in opposition to the romanticism of their predecessors.

Both sides were partly right. Customs vary from school to school and from age to age. In one school and at one period of the last century the new boy might meet with indifference,

at another with initiation. At all events, let no one suppose
that singing ceremonies were just an invention of authors who
knew nothing of the realities of school life. At some schools
these things figured prominently in the new fag's harassed
existence.

Rugby was one such school. 'Singing in Hall,' the official
historian and apologist admits, was a terrible ordeal for the
newcomer in the eighteen-thirties. Each new boy in turn had
to climb upon a table, with a candle in each hand, and do his
best to sing. 'If the trembling wretch made a false note, a
violent hiss followed; and all through the performance pellets
and crusts of bread were thrown at the boy or his candles,
often knocking the candles out of his hands and covering him
with tallow.' After the singing ordeal had finished, the victim
had to descend and pledge the House in a glass of salt and water,
flavoured with mustard and tooth powder, and stirred with a
tallow candle. He retired to his room, we are told, feeling
very uncomfortable.

The ceremony was long established, though the venue was
apt to change. A verse in the Rugby magazine for 1836 has a
line:

'When new boys on the pump were set to pelt at and to
sing.'

By the 'eighties the performance took place in the School
House, in one of the dormitories. After prayers, all those
who had been in the House for at least two years entered the
room, while the rest stood in a crowd in the doorway.

The new boy's ordeal had by this time been smoothed a
little. He was no longer a target for missiles and no longer
held his own candles; and after the singing he did not have to
soil his inside with foul concoctions. But the business could
still be an agony to a normally sensitive youngster. The victim
had to stand on an old bedstead, with two juniors as his
candle-bearers, so that every emotion on his young face was
revealed. If, through nervousness or lack of musical talent,
he failed to sing up effectively, his critical and outspoken

audience would not fail to let him know. If the disapproval was sufficiently general, then the whole crowd broke into a noisy chorus of 'Rule Britannia,' and the trembling singer was contemptuously dismissed. This, with a few slight changes, has remained the twentieth-century form of 'Lambsinging.'

Something similar used to take place at Shrewsbury, though here it was not so much an alarming ordeal to be endured once and then pushed behind, like a visit to the dentist to have a troublesome tooth extracted. The Shrewsbury 'Boxing and Singing' took place every Friday night, and new boys throughout their first year were compelled to take part if the master of ceremonies, impressively known as the Hall Constable, ordered them to do so.

'The singing' (we are told), 'was ridiculous. The wretched victim had to stand at the end of a long form in the centre of the Hall, surrounded by the crowd, a ribald, jeering audience, and he droned on until he was kicked over, form and all.' Even the unmusical child could not escape: if he could not sing he was commanded to hum, or at least produce some sort of noise. When the audience's chief purpose is to jeer the performer it does not, after all, matter very much what kind of performance he gives. The 'Boxing' which followed was not confined to new boys, and was called boxing only by courtesy.

There were many types of similar initiation ceremony, varying not only from school to school but from House to House within the school. At Eton the new Collegers who had to dwell in the Long Chamber were compelled to play themselves into the community by a feat of miniature mountaineering. An article was hidden away in a ventilator over the door, and new boys had to climb up the wooden partitions, as best they could, to fetch it. In the meantime they were furiously assailed in the rear with hand and fist. Following this, they were introduced to 'salt-beer' and then to 'Chamber singing.' This was in the 'seventies, and no doubt the ceremony lasted a good deal longer. In earlier days, to be put in Long

Chamber was often very like being sentenced to penal servitude in the galleys under a gang of savage task-masters; but this experience will be examined in a later chapter.

At Winchester, the ceremony was more elaborate. On the third Sunday of each 'half' (the illogical name for a term) every new boy in the House had to go to St Catherine's Hill, climb the chalk pit facing the town, then run round the maze on top of the hill. After this he was blindfolded, put in the middle of a clump of trees, and left to find his own way out. Having extracted himself, he was ordered to take a stone from the chalk pit, run down the hill, kiss the stone, and place it on the Domum Cross. But by the beginning of this century the custom had already begun to die out, and was not observed in every House.

Shrewsbury, in addition to its not very desirable Boxing and Singing, had one of the earliest new-boy ceremonies of the right type, in the form of New Boys' Races in School Gardens. The races were of no importance whatever as sporting contests, and brought no prizes to the visitors. But they were mainly free from the taint of bullying, and they gave the new boys the much-needed feeling that they were really taking part in something, and to that extent helped their self-esteem.

Sometimes the initiation was straightforward achievement. At Fettes, for example, Arthur Findlay found, in the 'nineties, that what he had to do was to turn a somersault over a wooden beam, about six feet up, which was stretched across his cubicle in the dormitory. As he was fairly athletic this did not worry him. What did embarrass him, on the occasion, was that he was equipped with the old-fashioned nightshirt—an unsuitable garb for somersaulting—whereas everyone else in the dormitory was wearing pyjamas.

Sometimes the desire to stress the new boy's inferiority remained the keynote of the ceremony. At one day school known to me it is the custom, even today, for the newcomers to be blooded by being shoved into the bushes at the edge of the school field. Harmless enough; and yet there is something wrong with the spirit behind it. Boys in a good school—and this one is by no means a bad grammar school—ought not to feel the need to assert their superiority over the newcomers. The attitude is the 'tin gloves' attitude, ruthlessly tamed, but not transformed into something inherently better.

Is the desire for some kind of initiation ceremony an essential need among the boys? I don't think it is; it has been pretty widespread, but some schools have got along without anything of the kind. Where the need is felt, however, a wise master has sometimes steered it into a sensible course. One public school housemaster, for example, has instituted a ceremony of 'Ringing in the New Boys,' in which the newcomers are formally welcomed in a friendly spirit instead of being made the butt of their seniors. It is at any rate a step in the right direction.

The boarding-school, by its nature, offers greater facilities for new-boy tormenting than the day school. But it would be wrong to pass over without comment the success with which even day boys manage to make it clear to a youngster fresh to the school that he is presumptuous in venturing to tread where they have trod. A daily train journey has always been particularly helpful, the railway compartment being, as it were, a temporary miniature boarding-house. Readers of Geoffrey Dennis's novel, *Bloody Mary's*, will recall how the two nine-year-old new boys to Queen Mary's Grammar School have to undergo a twenty-minute ordeal of strap thrashing and other bullying by members of a Gang who travel to and fro on the same train. This is fiction, from which I draw material reluctantly, but the experiences bear the stamp of absolute authenticity. Moreover they are analagous to the sufferings of S. P. B. Mais at Heath Grammar School, Halifax, at about the same period. 'My memory of that school (he wrote) is of the daily nightmare of being suffocated under cushions in the train that took us from Gretland to Halifax.'

Then there is H. E. Bates, who in 1916 obtained a scholarship from an elementary school to the grammar school at Kettering, and went there expecting everything to be terribly serious and on a high academic plane.

The first day shocked him into a different view. Like Abel Carey in *Bloody Mary's*, he had to travel to his school by train, and he found himself in the same compartment with some boys already established at Kettering Grammar School. One of them, 'a sinister gentleman with a club-foot and very black eyebrows and a dark smear of moustache, asked me my name, what my father did, whether I smoked, ordered me to call him sir, and then proceeded to knock me flat on my face in the carriage seat, and chastise my behind with a ruler.' When Bates tried to stand up he was knocked down again. By the time the bully had finished, Bates was in a sorry state, dusty and dishevelled. Other boys now joined in. One of them knocked him down once more, he was deliberately trampled on, and then thrashed with a window strap.

Even when there is no train journey it is still possible at a day school for older boys to express unwelcome, as Sir Osbert Sitwell found when he was sent for a short while to a day grammar school at Scarborough in 1902. Presumably it had leaked out that his father was Sir George Sitwell; possibly his nervousness and shyness made him seem more supercilious than he felt. But as soon as he arrived in the playground he was set upon by a crowd of bigger boys 'with whirling fists and yells of "Don't think you're everybody just because your father's a bloody baronet!" ' He returned from what he calls his first encounter with triumphant British democracy 'suffering from two black eyes, an aching body, and a sore heart.' Eric Gill, who was at a prep school in Brighton, repeats the familiar story: 'I remember my first day very vividly because in the playground one of the bigger boys almost, as it felt, twisted my arm off.'

It is natural for us to ask ourselves why it is that freshness and shyness have usually been so unfavourably received within school gates. The first part of the answer is, no doubt, that to some natures weakness offers scope for natural sadism, and the new boy, especially the shy one, is an obvious target. Bewildered by the strangeness of his surroundings, he is the unlikeliest victim to hit back. But beyond this youthful brutality, there is the desire, even among boys who are not naturally very sadistic, to bolster up their own anxiety to be in the swim by stressing and exaggerating the absence of this much-desired quality where it is most obviously absent. The inquisitor and tormentor of the new boy feels himself very much one of the lads.

Thus far the attitude is natural enough, and as a rule, in modern times, the note of unwelcome is not very harsh. But whether it shows itself in 'tin gloves' and roasting, or whether (as I am persuaded is commoner today) it is revealed less in positive brutality than in a tendency to ignore the newcomer completely or at any rate to tease him only a little, the attitude remains an undesirable one which schoolmasters have rarely done as much as they could and should to dissolve. Pupils are usually amenable to reasonable suggestion; and one of the things that a good school should teach is how to offer a civilised reception to those who are ill at ease.

CHAPTER TWO

BOYS WILL BE BOYS

IT was dangerous in the eighteenth century to annoy a
public schoolboy. Edmund Curll, a notorious literary
pirate and an enemy of Pope, was rash enough, early in
the century, to print without permission some portions of a
public speech by the captain of Westminster School. There was
no legal remedy in the days before the law of copyright.
Cudgel and fist were the common answers; and Westminster
did not hesitate to use them. Mr Curll was unwise enough to
let himself be spotted in the neighbourhood of Dean's Yard,
adjoining the school. He was immediately seized, given a
thorough blanket-tossing, dragged into the school and thrashed,
and then forced to go down on his knees and ask the mighty
captain's pardon.

Curll, it is true, was the sort of rogue who was not accustomed
to respectful treatment from anybody, but he was not the only
victim. Some sixty years later, in 1779, the same spirit still
prevailed. A man was violently assaulted in Dean's Yard by
six Westminster scholars, who 'beat and wounded him in a
most shocking manner, and after that Kelly (one of them),
with a drawn knife in his hand said, "If you don't kneel down
and ask pardon I will rip you up!"' The man was compelled
to submit to save his life.

This sort of action was regarded as high-handed, even for
Westminster boys, and the case came up for trial. The charges
were fully proved, and four of the boys were sentenced,
lightly enough, to a month's imprisonment with a fine of £25
each, unless they consented to ask the prosecutor's pardon.
This they refused to do. The course of justice, however, was

easily diverted. The father of one of the boys pleaded that his son would lose his place at Oxford University if the sentence were carried out, so the magistrates obligingly revised their verdict and a fine of £50 was substituted.

Schoolboys in the days of duelling were quick to take offence, and reckless in expressing irritation. The statutes of some old-established schools actually laid down regulations to guard against too ready a use of weapons. 'No scholar being at School may wear any dagger, hanger, or other weapon invasive, nor bring into the school staff or bat, except their meat knife.' Any boy who attacked the Master or another boy, was suspended for a month, and if he repeated the offence three times he was expelled.

This was at Manchester; but the South was equally violent. At Christ's Hospital, London (as Pepys once complained to the Governors), two of the bigger boys, who had the previous week been carried home dead drunk, started a drunken quarrel in the dining-hall of the Girls' Ward, drew swords, and had to be forcibly separated. One was the school captain.

By the nineteenth century weapons were used a little less freely than they had been in earlier days. But they were not unknown, and rough behaviour was if anything even commoner. When Dr Arnold was a boy at Winchester he was out for a walk one day with a group of others, in charge of a prefect, when they came upon a group of young trees. Just for fun they started pulling and hacking them down. A soldier's wife remonstrated with them, whereupon they put the point of a bayonet to her breast and threatened to stab her. Arnold himself, as we might expect, was shocked, but the prefect afterwards bragged about the incident as though it were something to be proud of.

Woe betide residents and passers-by on the stage-coach route when public schoolboys were returning home for the holidays. The young gentlemen, according to a Shrewsbury complainant, 'would use a coachman's whip about them most lustily,' and when their victims were out of reach of the whip would pelt them with stones. Nor would staying indoors necessarily bring safety. The boys thought nothing of throwing stones and firing bullets at house-windows as they passed.

Harrow was a particularly dangerous school for stone-throwing. When the London and North-Western Railway was being constructed near the school, the labourers employed on the work were regularly stoned as they walked through the town to buy food. The school had a 'sport' of its own known as 'Toozling.' Two (or more) boys would go to a field and walk one on each side of a hedge. As soon as a little bird was seen to fly into the hedge the boys approached cautiously until they had the bird exactly between them. They had already filled their pockets with stones, and they now began to throw vigorously and simultaneously. 'The poor bird usually became confused and rarely flew out; he was killed, often after the first two or three shots; and sometimes, if he flew out and in again along the hedge, the same toozle lasted ten or fifteen minutes. The sport was very exciting.' (I am, of course, quoting a Harrovian.)

Nor were birds the only victims of Harrow's ideas of sport. No dog, it was said, could live in the streets near the school. Some of the boys did, indeed, keep dogs, but merely as cat-killers. Cats were bought or stolen and carried in bags to a convenient field, where they were released in order to be chased and worried to death by the dogs. A similar pastime was to take ducks to Stanmore Pool or Elstree Reservoir so that they could be hunted by dogs.

Badger-baiting had long been a 'sport' of Eton boys. As early as 1761 a small boy wrote to his father: 'I was out badger-baiting last night, on Eaton Common. We worried one to death almost with the dogs, then turned out another which was very big. At last it broke its cord, and we ran it about a mile over hedges and ditches and gates and stiles, and finished our sport at eight o'clock, and did not kill it, but it is to be hunted again with a pack of hounds.' Well into the nineteenth century badger-baits, dog-fights, cat and duck hunts, and even bull-baiting were organised by or for the benefit of Eton boys in the fields near Windsor.

It is only fair to the young gentlemen of Eton and Harrow to add that they did not confine their annoyances to dogs, cats, birds, and navvies. A favourite amusement at the latter school was to rub out the hire numbers chalked on hired carriages driven out by Londoners, and substitute others; and there was always the popular game of throwing things at passers-by. A boy in one House, seated at an open window, saw some holiday-making Londoners in white flannels walking below. He deliberately threw an open bottle of ink at them. When the victims angrily abused him, he hurled every article in the room at their heads, including several lumps of coal and the fire-irons.

Nor was Eton much behind its rival. An eighteenth-century foreign visitor to England records how the habits of the Eton boys struck him . . . almost literally struck him. 'As we sailed up the Thames from Windsor to Eton, at about fifty paces from the College, we came to the head of a mill-bank, where were three of the grown scholars, who had hid themselves among the reeds, to erect a little battery. We passed by them and were saluted by a general discharge, which would doubt-less have peppered us most terribly if they had been better marksmen.' Fifty years later the game was still in progress, bargees being the particular victims, as indeed they had been for many years. An Old Etonian who had been at school in the eighteen-twenties afterwards described how at one bend in the river a wharf of rounded stones, taken from the bed of the river, had been laid down, 'lying there most invitingly.' This became the open armoury of the College. 'Fast and furious was the storm of stones hailed down from it on every poor barge that chanced to pass while we were in presence. Oaths and execrations were delicious music in our ears.'

Perhaps it was as well that the boys did not think of using even heavier artillery, as an Eton boy in the early nineteen-hundreds once did. In this case, however, the performance seems to have been due less to malicious purpose than to eccentricity. In Cannon Yard stood an ancient relic of the Crimean War. The boy, a young Scottish chieftain, had secretly filled this with an extraordinary miscellaneous assortment of missiles, including buttons, toothbrushes, and old boots. Somehow he contrived to add gunpowder in the appropriate place; and then, during the calling of Absence in the Yard, he gave himself the command to fire. The result was spectacular. There was a tremendous explosion, accompanied, according to an eye-witness, 'by a long, spluttering, popping fizzle, an apocalyptic rushing of flame, wind, and soot,' and an alarming discharge of the various projectiles. Hats were blown from the heads of startled spectators, and a dignified mortar-board from the head of the officiating master.

It may have been the war-fever inspired by the South African War that prompted this artillery escapade. The war, at any rate, was responsible for some explosive outbursts. For instance, in the autumn of 1899, when Mafeking and Ladysmith were being besieged by the Boers, and troopships were sailing eagerly for Durban, a boy at Hastings Grammar School one day whipped out a pocket-pistol and plugged a hole in the gymnasium door. He was successfully disarmed and soon afterwards dismissed. About the same time another boy at the same school also produced a pistol in class, though the only damage he did with it was to drill a hole through his own hand.

This was by no means the last instance of firearms in school. A master was shot and wounded by a pupil in a secondary school in North London during the last war; and in 1952, over six years after war had ceased to be an everyday reality in England, a Luger pistol went off in the desk of one London schoolboy and wounded another in the thigh.

The public-house scenes of Dean Farrar's oft-ridiculed *Eric or Little by Little* were not, as is sometimes supposed, the

B

result of an old fogey in a cathedral close allowing his imagination to run riot. Farrar, it is always worth remembering, was in his day and in his own way a brilliant schoolmaster. In spite of a sentimentalising tendency which at times damped his pages, he knew better than most of his critics what he was writing about. Drunkenness, and the vices which often go with it, were far from uncommon in eighteenth and early nineteenth-century schools, and to break bounds in order to slip off to the chosen pub was almost an accepted part of a boy's education.

At Eton in the late seventeenth century there was no gate-keeper—an invitation to crime which, as the Provost of the time complained, the pupils readily accepted, regardless of the headmaster, whoever he might be. 'In Mr Rosewell's time the schollers had frequently bottles of wine drawn up to their windows in baskets (though they are lockt in) . . . In Dr Roderick's time they got a false key to their own door, and went four or five abroad at midnight, for which severall were expelled.' Even the provision of a porter at the gate, however, was no defence against determined drinkers. A hundred years later lower boys were being sent to the notorious *Christopher*, at their own peril, to fetch cases of beer; and a bar in the Lower Chamber was loosened so that provisions could be passed through late at night.

'The rioting, masquerading, and drinking that took place in College after the doors were closed at night,' said an Old Etonian of the eighteen-twenties, 'can scarcely be credited.'

In the middle of the century the headmaster succeeded in having the *Christopher* closed. But rowdy behaviour still continued, especially in a badly-run House, as Gilbert Coleridge indicates—he himself belonging to a more refined House opposite.

'A novel form of booby-trap was instituted one day at Rouse's. A canister of gunpowder was placed on the table, a bath placed over the canister, and various pieces of furniture piled on the bath. When the occupant of the room was approaching, the fuse was lit. The result was an explosion, a wreck of the room, and a great hole in the ceiling. We were accustomed at all seasons to hear strange sounds from over the way. Far into the night the popping of corks and the sound of revelry would ascend into the starlit sky, and the lilt of choruses so Rabelaisian that our ancient maid used to declare that "sich things ought to be stopped," an opinion with which some of us, still smarting from fractured windows for which we had to pay, smashed pictures, and broken sleep, cordially agreed.'

Even in the less violent Houses, so another Old Boy tells us, 'smoking and drinking were far from rare among the boys. Beer was smuggled into the Houses from "Tap," a drinking-bar in the High Street, and many a nightly pipe was smoked after the housemaster had gone his rounds.'

At Harrow, early in the nineteenth century, there existed a 'Red Nightcap Club,' generally regarded as the 'Hell-fire Club' of Harrow. 'Drunkenness and dissipation,' we are told by an ardent Harrovian, 'sank deep into the social life of Harrow during the first forty years of the century,' inspired, it may be, by the example of George IV. Many Old Harrovians would not send their sons to the school, so black was its reputation.

At Winchester it was a regular thing for disreputable tradesmen to carry sweets and cakes to St Catherine's Hill to sell to the boys on their walks and half-holiday excursions, and to engage at the same time in the profitable trade of selling brandy in ginger-beer bottles.

Westminster School, with its extreme proximity to London's gayest night life, offered obvious temptations to its scholars, one of the strongest being theatre visits. George Colman the Elder, the notable playwright and theatre-manager of the late eighteenth century, was always ready to welcome any schoolfellows of his son at Covent Garden or the Haymarket; and in due course Colman the Younger followed his father's example. At one of the Houses a convenient lamp-iron fixed in the wall provided a useful foothold for departing and returning boys. The Earl of Albemarle recounts how, returning after one summer vacation, he found the top of the wall had been raised and broken glass inserted. The answer, he found, was a rope-ladder and a dummy figure in his bed, with the aid of which he remained an unofficial theatregoer until he was expelled.

Westminster's main interest, however, was fighting. The big fight is the main scene in countless school stories; while John Ridd *v*. Robin Snell, Cuff *v*. Dobbin, and Tom Brown *v*. Slogger Williams are among the classic scenes in famous novels. Art in this respect was true to life, for in the days of prize-fighting, fists were freely used at almost every school. But there never was such another school for fighting as Westminster.

The traditional fighting-ground was in the very shadow of the Abbey, in the so-called 'Green' enclosed by the cloisters. The contests, as at many other schools, were carried on in the style of the professional prize-fights, with a second taking his champion on his knee between rounds, rubbing his hands, and offering good advice. The fight usually lasted until one of the combatants was too battered and exhausted to continue, and was a gruesome spectacle to the child unused to such affairs. 'I felt sick at the sight of blood pouring down from so many wounds,' a boy wrote after seeing his first battle. But hardened spectators were less sensitive, and their excited shouting often disturbed the services in the adjacent Abbey.

So accepted a part of school life were these battles that not only were the two opponents themselves easily able to obtain time off from school to hammer each other in the Fighting Green, but any friends who wanted to see the fight could usually receive permission also. An attempt by Southey's headmaster, Dr Vincent, to compel the school to desert the cloisters and go into school before an exciting fight was over led ultimately to a two-day rebellion in 1791.

William Carey, who became headmaster shortly after Vincent's retirement, was more accommodating, having himself been a fighter in his time. A boy in trouble for laziness might yet retrieve his position by his fists. An idle boy named Lambert was one day being discussed by the headmaster and the Captain of the School, and the usual remedy for bad work seemed likely to be applied. Then Carey noticed that the boy had a black eye.

'How did he get that?' he asked.

'Fighting a town boy.'

'Who won?'

'Lambert.'

'Ah well,' said the headmaster, 'if he's a good fighter we mustn't be too hard on him for his Latin and Greek.'

When it was first founded in 1843, Marlborough was a school with a strong fighting bias, partly because organised games were non-existent. One of its first pupils remembered a fight between two of the biggest fellows which lasted a full hour. It ended in a draw, with both combatants being taken off to the sick-room. On another occasion a tough fighter battered a bigger opponent into temporary blindness, and still remained on his own feet, though he was so weak through exhaustion and loss of blood that a friend had to cut up his meat at dinner. Authority at this school did not look favourably on fighting (though it was remarkably tolerant towards bullying), and the freely-used cane was apt to add to the wounds inflicted on each other by two pugilists.

Occasionally a school fight has proved fatal. At Hitchin Grammar School many years ago one boy accidentally killed another by a blow on the nose. But the most shocking instance was a fight at Eton in 1825, which receives only a discreetly casual reference in the school's official history. I tell the story here a little more fully.

Two boys had words one day over the possession of a seat in the schoolroom. They began to scrap, but were separated by the Captain of the School and agreed to a formal fight later on. One boy, C. A. Wood, was a good deal taller than the other, Ashley-Cooper minimus (a son of the sixth Earl of

Shaftesbury), though whether he was older was a matter for subsequent dispute.

The battle duly took place, an older boy, Alexander Leith, having been asked by Ashley-Cooper major, the eldest brother, to act as second. For a few rounds Cooper managed to hold his own. But in the eighth, ninth, and tenth rounds he became weak and exhausted. It was evident that he was not a match for his bigger opponent, and the contest should clearly have been stopped.

Far from throwing in the towel, the youngster's backers offered him artificial recuperation in the form of brandy, a fair quantity of which had been brought to the field. Before the eleventh round Leith gave him a good dose. Subsequently he asserted that he told Cooper just to wash his mouth out with it. However that may be, a good deal of it went down the boy's throat, and revived him sufficiently for him to go on fighting pluckily. Delighted at the effectiveness of this energy-restorer, the backers of both contestants plied their men with frequent doses between the rounds.

The battle had started at four o'clock. They were still fighting an hour later. At one stage in the contest Cooper received a blow on the temple which felled him to the ground, where he lay for fully half a minute. Some of the boys were afraid that this was going to stop the fun; some (though apparently they kept silent) may even have felt that it ought to be stopped. But there was plenty of brandy still left in the bottles, and presently the battered loser was able to continue. At least he had the satisfaction of knowing, if he was conscious of anything at all, that his opponent was pretty exhausted also; which was not surprising seeing that they had by this time fought over fifty rounds.

About the sixtieth round, when they had been battling for just under two hours, the smaller boy collapsed and fell heavily on his head. The fight was over, and brandy no longer had any power to revitalise an insensible fourteen-year-old boy.

The victim's two elder brothers carried him back to the

A fight in the 'forties at Marlborough

boarding-house of the Rev. Mr Knapp, himself a keen follower of prize-fighting, but seemingly engaged on his own pursuits elsewhere during the whole of this afternoon and evening. No other master or senior was in charge of the House during his absence in these very casual days; there was only a woman servant with no authority.

She at least had a little more sense than the boys. When the unconscious loser was carried in and put to bed she asked his brothers whether she had better send for the doctor.

'There's no need to,' said Ashley-Cooper major. 'He's fast asleep. He'll be all right when he wakes up.'

But he was not fast asleep. He was in a dying coma; and when, some hours later, somebody thought that medical assistance had better be sought after all, it was too late. The boy died just after the doctor's arrival.

There was, of course, an inquest; and rarely has any responsible body of people been slower to respond then the Eton authorities. An understandable but ill-judged eagerness to keep things hushed up overshadowed every other aim. One of the masters, Mr Okes, had to be fetched to the coroner's court by a constable before he would consent to give the Christian name of the dead boy's second in the fight.

Wood was charged with manslaughter, but eventually acquitted on the ground that the contest was conducted in accordance with the rules of regular prize-fights.

Outside opinion was naturally unfavourable to Eton, *The Times*, among other voices, being quite outspoken. A day was to come when this great journal would have Etonian connexions and would point its barbs at Harrow; but its present owner had been at the Merchant Taylors School and its editor was an Old Blue. They stressed three points as being particular causes of uneasiness. The first was the free administration of brandy to the boy combatants. The second was the appalling ignorance of the boys 'at this distinguished place of education' in being unable to recognise the difference between sleep and insensibility caused by violence. Thirdly, there was 'the want of discipline in this eminent school . . . It is really monstrous that a boy should lie in a dying state from six o'clock till ten in the house of a person who has undertaken the moral as well as the classical charge of him.'

To this criticism Eton had no real answer; but instead of owning up honourably to a serious dereliction of duty she did her best to brazen it out. Dr Keate, the headmaster, blamed the upper boys (not without justice) for not stopping the fight, and disclaimed all responsibility in the matter, which was, he implied, one of those little misfortunes which are liable to happen in the best regulated schools. He commended Lord Shaftesbury for not prosecuting, and then proudly exhibited the coffin to the boys, as if young Ashley-Cooper had died bravely fighting for his country.

Dr Hawtrey, at this time the Lower Master, tried to pass the buck away from the school altogether. Three gentlemen riding home from a Hunt had stopped for a few minutes to look on at the contest. They, Hawtrey protested feebly, were the guilty men for not breaking up the battle; though why three passing strangers should be expected to interfere in Eton boys' activities when the masters held aloof it is difficult to see.

The classic fatuity in this distresssing case, however, was an utterance by the coroner. A boy witness, who presumably had seen what was happening, asserted that young Ashley-Cooper drank about half a pint of brandy during the course of the fight.

'Nonsense,' exclaimed the coroner. 'He could not possibly have drunk so much neat brandy. Why, that would have been sufficient to have killed him!'

In spite of these mishaps, it may be argued that learning to fight under some form of restraint, even the limited restraint of the Prize Ring, was a useful accomplishment. Though a boy might fail to learn much Latin and Greek from his master —and there was rarely anything else to learn in school—at least he picked up from his schoolfellows the art of attack and defence.

Another subject on the unofficial curriculum was swearing, and Westminster, again, specialised in this. When Lord John Russell first went to the school in 1803 at the age of eleven, some bigger boys ordered him, as a very junior fag, to ask a glazier to mend a broken window in the boarding-house. The glazier failed to appear. 'Did you swear at him?' the boys asked Russell. He had to admit that he hadn't. 'Then go and swear at him,' they ordered.

Blundell's was another school noted for its interest in living language as opposed to the dead languages studied in the school-room. When little Frederick Temple (afterwards headmaster of Rugby and Archbishop of Canterbury) went there in 1834 he was horrified.

'The boys swear so much that I can hardly bear it; and they not only do it themselves, but they take away my things and then say I may not have them again unless I swear, which of course I will not do.'

Kipling tended to excuse the foul language at his own school, the United Services College, Westward Ho, with the assertion that it was something a boy ought to learn early and then put away by the time he was seventeen. But there are surely few things that a boy forgets so reluctantly as bad language.

In spite of its foul language, the school, Kipling claimed 'was clean with a cleanliness that I never heard of in any other school. I remember no cases of even suspected perversion.'

This is a matter which it is not easy to discuss because it was so rarely referred to before Alec Waugh, in 1917, shocked his own school in particular and the public school world in general by the publication of his youthful *Loom of Youth*. It is not improbable that this vice has grown commoner during the last hundred years, for precisely the reason that bullying and general hooliganism have grown less common and privacy commoner. There was probably little scope for homosexual practices when boys lived a communal life in which the accepted thing to do with smaller boys was to fag and bully them without mercy.

The only references in earlier years are oblique and uncertain.

'With regard to the Vice which you speak of as taking place in College,' wrote the father of a Westminster boy to his son in 1824, 'God grant that you may feel the same abhorrence of it as you express in your letter.' But in the absence of the boy's own letter we cannot be sure whether the father is referring to sexual perversion, swearing, or looking at naughty pictures.

Perhaps the first direct mention (though even this is oblique enough) occurs in an article by the headmaster of Clifton College in 1881. 'It must be believed that immorality, used in a special sense which I need not define, has been of late increasing among the upper classes in England.' The increase, of course, coincided with the growth in popularity of the public boarding-school; and the problem is essentially (though not quite exclusively) a boarding-school problem. It has been described as 'the boarding-school master's nightmare,' with particular reference to headmasters and housemasters. One reason for the tremendous emphasis on 'healthy games'— compulsory cricket or football several times a week, and no slacking—has been the master's desire to leave no room for anything else. 'My prophylactic against certain unclean microbes was to send the boys to bed dead tired,' the headmaster of the United Services College admitted to his most distinguished Old Boy. The same instinct, it seems, appears in girls' schools. 'Run about *like* boys, and then you won't think *of* them' was the principle (unspoken of course) on which the Sherborne School for Girls was conducted, Miss Arnot Robertson has assured us.

At Gresham's School, Holt, boys were put on their honour not to do or say anything indecent—successfully up to a point, but as they were expected to confess to their lapses and to report those of others, the system bristled with psychological dangers. At many schools there were no locks on the

lavatory doors, as a precaution against the smallest rooms in
the school being used as a refuge by homosexuals. At Malvern,
and no doubt at other schools, there were no doors at all.
At Charterhouse the cubicles in the dormitories had partitions
electrically wired so that an alarm was raised if a boy tried
to make his way into another boy's cubicle.

But even the most efficient alarm bells cannot function
comprehensively. Boys are not always in their cubicles, and
the more desperately schoolmasters watch for undesirable
practices and try to chain up the instincts which promote them,
the more these practices are likely to flourish one way or
another. So it was at Charterhouse, on the evidence of Charles
Graves. He had been three weeks at the school, and found himself drawn against a much older boy in the House Squash
Rackets Competition. 'I was pink and white,' he says, 'thirteen,
fairish-haired with blue-grey eyes, ideal material for what
was called in those days "a house-tart." ' He was too innocent
to know what was happening when his opponent put down
his racket and began to fumble with him. 'All I knew was that
something ugly was in the air.' He hit out, and the other boy
struck his head against the wall of the court and was knocked
out.

Graves did not achieve popularity as a heroic defender of
his honour. On the contrary his prudishness was generally
frowned upon by the other boys.

There is some evidence that this particular vice is as strong
today as it ever was, in spite of increased sex education.
Recent correspondence in the educational press has brought
to light some disturbing facts. Homosexual activity was said
by more than one writer, drawing on personal knowledge,
to be widespread, since the war as well as between the wars.
What was perhaps even more disturbing than this positive
evidence was the attitude of a clerical headmaster leaping to
the defence of the boarding-school. 'Boys are no longer afraid
to talk quite freely about sex with their housemasters or tutors,'
he assured us genially; and added that they would be willing

to talk equally freely to any visitor who wished to question them. Such blindness to the nature of the normal reticent boy leaves one uneasy.

Closely linked with the question of sex is the matter of indecency. It produces curious anomalies in school, as it does in society. (One can openly undress on the beach but not in the street.) The curiously public arrangement of some school lavatories has already been referred to. Contrasted with this is the odd prudery over nudity which existed at some schools as late as this century. At Rugby, for instance, a boy changing after games had to do so with the aid of a towel carefully draped around his waist, just as if he were bathing on an open beach. Not many boys' schools, I think, shared this delicacy, which was no legacy from Dr Arnold's robuster days; but at least one girls' convent school (and no doubt it is not alone) has surpassed it. At the Catholic School of Lippington the girls were not allowed to see even their own bodies, and had to take their bi-weekly baths not only behind locked doors in private and separate bathrooms but also swathed in huge calico cloaks from neck to toe. This, at any rate, was the rule as late as 1914.

The problem of theft is common to all types of school, from Primary to Public. A certain amount of 'pinching' is so common that it would be pedantic to threaten it with solemn denunciation. Respect for other people's property, especially eatables, is not a characteristic schoolboy attribute. How many boys are there who have never taken another boy's pencil or ruler, or held on to a book belonging to the school? (It should no doubt be added that although there is safety in numbers there is no virtue in them.)

Stealing money is another matter. Most pupils would draw the line here; though I know schools in certain districts where even the headmaster dares not leave his study without first locking the door.

Ardent churchmen are apt to assure us that religious instruction is the answer to this petty lawlessness. Alas, the facts do not support them. When Marlborough College was opened in 1843 it was intended primarily for the benefit of the clergy, and the bulk of its pupils were clergymen's sons. In theory, its light should have so shone before other schools that they would have seen its good work, and followed suit. In fact, however, in its earliest years the school had few rivals for sheer blackguardism. The notorious bullying which was practised does not concern us at the moment; but, in addition, there were few schools where it was more unsafe to allow a private titbit to be observed by the other boys.

Edward Lockwood, who at the age of eight was one of its first pupils, recounts how, being given half-a-crown one day, he was persuaded by a glib shopman into laying it out on a store of jam tarts. He was at once pursued by a horde of boys. When he timidly, but perhaps unwisely, refused to give them one each, and put the treasures in his desk, he and his desk were sent flying, and the store of tarts vanished without his tasting even one. Shocked by this episode he had a play-box made, with lock and key. He himself had nothing to put in it, since half-crown tips were rare compliments; but he lent it to a young friend who had received a hamper of apples. Both boys soon discovered that it takes more than wood and locks to defeat the predatory instinct of clergymen's sons. A mass of boys swarmed round the box, and in a few minutes the two eight-year-olds were left lying in the playground, with the remnants of a shattered play-box beside them, and a few crushed apples the only evidence of its former contents.

The little boys of Christ's Hospital, London, used to endure a systematic piracy. The bigger boys would wait at the gates as the youngsters returned after a half-holiday, laden with cakes and fruit, and with silver coins jingling in their pockets. When they reached the gates they would be forced to pay toll, and would be lucky if they reached their beds at night with even a memento of what they had brought from home.

One of the most curious examples of schoolboy iniquity occurred in the eighteen-twenties at Lewisham School, the forerunner of the present Caterham School. A small band of delinquents developed the habit of robbing the school orchard and stealing food and money from other pupils' lockers. This was not an unusual schoolboy crime, but the leader of the gang was less ordinary. 'In plundering, blasphemy, and murderous principles,' the headmaster asserted, 'he seems to have attained a perfection rarely to be paralleled in one of his age.'

'One day,' this criminal admitted in his confession, 'I said to my friend, "Suppose I was to make a bargain with the Devil? Then we could go into the orchard without being seen." ' With blood drawn from a deliberately cut finger he wrote the Lord's Prayer backwards. Then came the written compact.

'I make a league with thee, O Devil, if thou wilt give me a ring to produce any earthly thing for me and my friend for two years.'

Young Faustus himself was bold enough to abjure his prayers, but his friend had timid scruples.

'It will offend the Devil if you say them,' the leader insisted, so his fainter-hearted supporter compromised by just pretending.

Perhaps the Devil was offended after all, for he did not protect his youthful adherents. The leader suffered the fullest extremity of school law. The Committee, to whom the headmaster had to refer serious offences, decided emphatically that there was nothing for it but immediate expulsion. 'His case,' they declared, 'is of a peculiarly aggravated and awful nature, which implies in a person of his age unusual depravity and guilt.'

Nobody, it seems, sat back and had a good laugh at these young traffickers in Black Magic—unless perhaps it was the Devil.

CHAPTER THREE

IN THEIR LITTLE NESTS

'**B**oy!' shouted a harsh master to a sobbing new blue-coat pupil named Samuel Taylor Coleridge, 'the School is your Father! Boy, the School is your Mother! Boy, the School is your Brother! The School is your Sister! The school is your first-cousin, and your second-cousin, and all the rest of your relations! Let's have no more crying!'

The Rev. James Boyer was not, on this occasion, acting the tyrant. His intention may even have been relatively kindly. He was stating a fact to which the homesick newcomer had got to accustom himself. A boy sent off to a boarding-school does not attend school: he is swallowed up by it.

In days when masters did not regard it as any part of their duties to supervise the out-of-schoolroom practices of their pupils, and when they themselves, indeed, sometimes led the way in brutality, the child in his first years at school might well envy Jonah, whose swallowing was simple, painless, and brief.

Vicesimus Knox, later a capable and liberal-minded head-master of Tonbridge School, describes how the process affected him in the 1760's:

'I am confident that I derived some of the greatest vices and misfortunes of my life from a fashionable school (Merchant Taylors). I was placed there when I was but an infant, and lived as a fag under a state of oppression from my schoolfellows unknown to any slave in the plantations. Many hardships I suffered by day, but I would have borne them without complaint if I had been permitted to repose at night, and enjoy those sweet slumbers which my fatigue and my age invited;

but several nights in a week I was disturbed at various hours for the mere wantonness of cruelty, thrust out of bed, and, in the coldest weather, stripped of the clothes. My health and my growth, I have no doubt, were injured by the ill usage I suffered, and the constant fear in which I spent my infant days. I was beaten by the senior boys without the least reason. Before I was twelve years old . . . I suffered in mind and body more than many adult criminals who are convicted of flagrant violation of the laws of their country.'

'The eldest son,' says Southey writing of a playmate of his youth, 'was taken from the Charterhouse, because he was literally almost killed there by the devilish cruelty of the boys; they used to lay him before the fire till he was scorched, and shut him in a trunk with sawdust till he had nearly expired with suffocation. The Charterhouse at that time was a sort of hell upon earth for the younger boys.'

Southey himself went to Westminster, where to begin with he boarded with the usher of the Fifth Form. He was placed in a room with an older boy of ungoverned temper. On the slightest provocation this boy would throw a metal beer mug or a poker at his young companion, and used to pour water in his ear when he was asleep in bed. 'He once attempted to hold me by the leg out of the window; it was the first floor and over a stone area. Had I not struggled in time and clung to the frame with both hands, my life would probably have been sacrificed to this freak of temporary madness.'

The miseries experienced by little Frederick Reynolds when he first went to Westminster were endured mainly in the boarding-house of a Mrs Jones; and it was at this same establishment a year or two later that a highly sensitive Welsh boy was all but driven to death. 'Taffy slept in my room,' said Reynolds, 'and used frequently to declare that if his petty tyrants did not cease to torment him he would hang himself. This threat, constantly repeated without execution, naturally only led to increased ridicule and manual annoyance. At last, to my surprise and horror, he literally kept his word. One evening, suddenly entering our chamber, I discovered him hanging from the bed-post, black in the face, and in a state of suspended animation. I called for assistance, and several boys immediately arriving, one of them instantly cut the rope with his pocket-knife.'

At Shrewsbury, two centuries earlier, a boy of about twelve accomplished the same feat more successfully, and 'hanged himself in his chambre where he did lie.' 'He was an idle boy and hated the school,' the authorities recorded, wiping their consciences clean.

Such school tragedies, it must be added in order to avert educational complacency, are not entirely things of the past, though I do not suggest that the motives are necessarily the same. The sun is not always shining in schools today, nor is every pupil as happy as a lark. Less than ten years ago a seventeen-year-old boy attending a minor public boarding-school at a market town in a southern county shot himself through the head soon after the start of the autumn term. A year or two later (in 1952) a boy of fifteen, the son of one of the masters, hanged himself in the school chapel of a famous public school a few miles away. Even while this chapter was being written, a fourteen-year-old boy who (unusually) was competent at games but made unhappy by them, was found gassed in the kitchen of his home on the day he was due to return to his public boarding-school in Cornwall. A simple verdict was recorded that death was due to coal gas poisoning, the coroner observing that he had the gravest doubts as to the state of the boy's mind.

Man's inhumanity to man, it has been said, is nothing when compared with boy's inhumanity to boy; and un-supervised boarding-schools certainly gave unparalleled opportunities to the natural bully or the boy with at least a bullying streak. By the early nineteenth century some schools had become so notorious, even outside the school, that few parents would accept scholarships for their sons to live in College. Strange as it may seem, the most famous schools were among the worst, and the ancient foundations of Henry VI, William of Wykeham, and John Lyon, began to languish. /

'The lads underwent privations that would have broken down a cabin boy,' wrote Sir William Creasy of the dreaded Long Chamber where the Eton Collegers lived and slept, 'and which would have been thought inhuman if inflicted on a galley-slave.' Cotton Minchin, though an ardent Harrovian, records that a friend of his had a half-brother who died before he came of age, his constitution being completely undermined by the bullying he had received on the Hill in the 1820's. It was not surprising that many men who had been to Harrow would not send their sons to endure 'the blackguardism rampant on the Hill before the time of Vaughan.' Sydney Smith, who entered Winchester in 1781, used to shudder, even in his old age, at his recollections of it. 'The whole system,' he maintained, 'was one of abuse, neglect, and vice.' Many years later Cotton Minchin asked a distinguished Wykehamist who left the College in the 1860's whether there was much bullying in those days. 'Bullying?' was the answer. 'I'm almost inclined to ask—was there anything else?'

In the first half of the nineteenth century the College 'seemed stricken with decay . . . College and Commoners alike were on the down-grade,' as A. F. Leach, its official historian and almost fanatical supporter, admits; though he also claims that 'in the darkest days of Winchester, College never sank as it did at Eton, under the barbarous life of Long Chamber, where for many years the numbers did not rise above fifty.'

Long Chamber deserved its name as well as its reputation. It was 172 feet long and 27 feet wide. For two centuries all the seventy Scholars of Eton had to live in it, many of them two in a bed. Order, however, was preserved during this early period, for according to the official injunction, 'the School-master and Usher shall lodge in their chambers at the ends of the Long Chamber to prevent disorders which may otherwise happen.' How wise the injunction was became evident when it was disregarded. Early in the eighteenth century the Usher gave up his room at the end of Long Chamber (the Master had already gone), and the great dormitory was left to rule itself at night.

The outstanding feature of its self-rule was the absolute domination of the bully. Even the best seniors, however kindly in their own conduct, strictly observed the convention by which no Sixth Former interfered with another. 'The Captains of Long Chamber (and its small extensions) were good and merciful,' wrote A. D. Coleridge of the 1840's, 'but they winked at the ruffianism of my tormentor, who, as a Sixth Form boy, could do as he pleased.' The Captain of Lower Carter's Chamber, where there were only five boys, was 'one of the most fascinating and gifted collegers of the time,' but 'he never interfered to protect a small boy.'

One evening Coleridge's particular bully, who thought nothing of flogging his young victim for fun with a stolen birch-rod, 'took to battering a friend of mine about the head and face so savagely that the poor lad was kept in bed for days until his bruises healed. I was a witness of that performance, and shall not forget it to my dying day. I marvelled at the Sixth Form boys at their supper-table, conscious of all the brutality going on, and never lifting a finger to interfere.' Even the headmaster of the time, Dr Hawtrey, himself a most humane man, made no attempt to investigate, so strong was the convention that the boys must rule themselves. He preached eloquent sermons against bullying, but that was as far as it went.

Among the more orderly and regular torments that younger boys had to undergo was an operation known as 'Pricking for Sheriff.' The victim was placed face downwards across the lap of the chief executioner, the seat of his trousers being stretched as tight as possible. Pins were then stuck firmly and deliberately into the tightened seat, the small boy being warned that if he screamed louder than the previous victims he would receive an even worse penalty. 'Seeing the stars' was the name given to the familiar practice of tipping young sleepers suddenly out of bed. Even more familiar was blanket-tossing. In its more ceremonial form each junior was tossed six times while the tossers shouted a Latin incantation. But this kind of ceremony easily gets out of hand when there are unchecked bullies performing it, and there is little doubt that sometimes it became a serious terror to small boys. One boy, afterwards a tutor at Cambridge, had been so recklessly tossed, early in the century, that he struck his head when falling, was almost scalped, nearly lost his life, and remained disfigured for the rest of his days.

One of the evil absurdities of the system was that everyone who became a Colleger, no matter what position in the school he might have reached, was treated as a first-year 'fag' in Long Chamber. A. D. Coleridge recalls a Fifth Form Oppidan who took a scholarship to become a King's Scholar. He had always treated those below him with great kindness in his position as a fairly senior Oppidan; but when he entered College he was treated as a menial fag, and his life was made a misery. It was the delight of his less civilised fellow Collegers to hold him under the College pump, and in the winter to roll him in the snow in the Yard after supper.

The Long Chamber at Eton was probably the largest as well as the most fearsome of commonroom-dormitories. But many schools had quite big chambers for sleeping purposes, and as a rule they were used as commonrooms as well. Sometimes, later in the nineteenth century, they were divided into cubicles. At some schools, up to the 1830's the pupils slept two in a bed, single beds being charged as an extra.

The Westminster School Statutes of 1560 expressly lay down that 'all scholars shall spend the night in one or two chambers, two in a bed.' At Shrewsbury it was considered quite a luxury to have a single bed. The bedrooms here were smaller than at many schools, usually containing from four to six beds. F. A. Paley, who was at the school from 1826 to 1833, describes the bedroom he had when he first went there as being about sixteen feet square and containing five double beds; and he makes no mention of any later improvements. Single beds, however, did become the rule during the headmastership of B. H. Kennedy (1836–1867). At Christ's Hospital, Hertford (a branch of the more famous London school), the dormitories contained about twenty-five beds. 'In those days,' wrote an Old Blue in 1841, a few years after leaving, 'the beds were intended for two, but by a recent decision of the committee each boy has now a bed to himself.'

Single blessedness at night, then, was the general tendency at this period, and to most boys it no doubt seemed a great step forward in comfort. It is, however, worth noting that even double beds would have seemed a luxury to the pupils of the Choir School at Wells Cathedral, and no doubt to others. Here, according to a regulation of the 1400's, choristers had to sleep three in a bed, 'two small boys with their heads to the head of the bed, and one big one, who is to put his feet between the heads of the small ones.'

Whether the beds were single, double, or triple, the accommodation in famous schools was far from luxurious, and even the improvements that seeped in from time to time during the nineteenth century left the living conditions a good deal below what would now be thought tolerable in an exceptionally primitive youth hostel. Westminster may be taken as a fairly typical example. By the early nineteenth century the Scholars, who lived in the main school building, had advanced to single beds. The Old Dormitory had been replaced in 1730 by a new one, which in due course became as dilapidated as its predecessor. 'Life in College,' says a Westminster historian writing of the 1820's, 'was unbelievably rough. The boys slept and worked and played in one long room, unheated except by three open fires round which the seniors clustered to the exclusion of the smaller boys; and when preparations for the Play were going on, conditions were worse, the juniors being actually obliged to sleep under the stage.' A writer in 1880 describes the Dormitory as 'a long, lofty room with bare,

Toefitying at Winchester, also showing 'The Scheme'

whitewashed walls, partitioned off into cubicles for the sake of privacy, the furniture of these small cabins consisting of a little iron bedstead, a strip of carpet, and a dressing-table . . . It is at once unsightly, cold, dreary, and wholly unsuitable to the purposes of a sleeping-chamber. Rats, we are told, are even now not foreign to the spot.'

Eton's Long Chamber endured or enjoyed a similar visitation. Dozens of neck-of-mutton bones were discovered under the floor-boards in 1868. They had been used as bait to attract the rats, which the boys used to try to trap in long stockings, and then hang on the bed-posts.

It would be a mistake to suppose that primitive conditions inevitably brought misery to the boarders. Schoolboys normally have a happy way of making the best of things, and are not greatly affected by simple physical discomforts. 'When viewed in the daytime,' says a Wykehamist looking back to 1840, 'and devoid of its occupants, the dormitory is somewhat dreary; but when the boys are there, and the fire blazing, a great change comes over the scene . . . I can call to mind no scene so cosy and cheerful, especially when, having turned into bed after a hard day's work, I used drowsily to watch the darting flames till I gradually sank into dreams of a quiet home.'

The dreams, however, might be rudely interrupted. A favourite practice at Winchester during this period was what was known as 'Toefitying.' A loop of string was fastened by slip-knot to a boy's big toe, and then lustily pulled. Whether this was a foolish and painful practical joke or plain bullying would depend on the relations between the parties concerned. If it were a joke the victim would probably retaliate on the jester by flinging something at his head. To the bully there was, of course, no effective answer; though at Winchester the prefects seem to have been often readier to intervene than the Seniors at Eton, unless the Prefect himself happened to be the bully.

One big boy refined on the joke by fastening a loop to the toes of each of the other three or four boys in his chamber (excluding of course the prefects), attaching these lines to a single line which ran through a staple in the upright post in the centre of the room, and thence to a fishing-reel beside his own bed. He then proceeded to wind up the reel briskly until he had each boy standing on one leg facing the post, the other leg extended forward at right angles.

Besides offering scope for rough and ready schoolboy humour, 'toefitying' was used as an alarm clock. A boy in each chamber—needless to say, the smallest boy—was chosen to have his toe fastened to a line the other end of which was tied to a window-bar. A single boy could thus quietly wake the whole school if need be. All he had to do was to go out into the Quad, pull the string at each open window, and the 'toefitied' victim would then arouse the rest of his chamber in a less startling way.

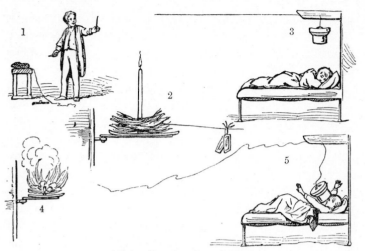

'The Scheme' at Winchester

Even this utilitarian practice could be exploited by the joker. An old Wykehamist, it is recorded, was one evening strolling in the Quad with a friend on the staff, a new master who had not been educated at Winchester. Presently the master left his friend for a short while in order to pay a visit to Third Chamber. The Old Boy noticed a string attached to the window-bar of this room, and when he judged that the right moment had come he pulled it firmly towards him. The result was that as the master moved into the centre of the room a boy suddenly shot out from one of the beds, flashed past him, hopping on one leg, and finished up with his other leg half out of the window. As the unfortunate victim was a stammerer it took the master a long time to get an explanation of this peculiar behaviour.

A more ingenious method of waking a junior, when the older occupants of the Chamber wished to be called early in order to study, was known as 'The Scheme.' 'The Functior (or rushlight) was known to burn at a certain rate—say an inch an hour. If it was lighted at nine o'clock, and we wanted to rise at four, seven inches only were allowed to protrude above the socket (the rest being cut off), around which a quantity of paper was arranged, and a string tied, which was carried through a hole in the top of a Junior's bed. To the end of this string a parcel of books, or a pint-cup of water was fastened. When the candle burnt down, it ignited the paper and burnt the string, causing the books (or water) to fall, which roused the sleeper, who proceeded to wake the rest.'

Unhappy Junior! Conditions were not alike at every school, but his life could often be a grim one, both within and without the dormitory. On cold nights he was commonly used as a bed-warmer by his seniors, having to lie between one pair of icy sheets until it pleased his fag-master to retire to bed, then being sent off, bleary-eyed, to his own icy sheets. He might consider himself lucky if he was allowed to retain his own bed-covering, for, as Lewis Carroll wrote of Rugby, 'the smaller boys' beds in winter were denuded of blankets that the bigger ones might not feel cold.'

These were not bullying acts, in the deliberate sense of the word, but were casual practices taken as a matter of course, with no particular ill will towards the junior concerned. Most schools, however, knew other ways in which Juniors might be exploited for the pleasure of their elders. Eton's Long Chamber had no monopoly of sadistic entertainment.

At Blundell's 'Bolstering' was a popular pastime on holidays. The big boys would beat down their bolsters hard at one end, and twist the loose part round and round to form a handle. Then a selected number of small boys (chosen for some pretended fault or just at the caprice of the bolsterers) would have to lie down one at a time on a bed to be mercilessly pummelled by five bolsterers, two on either side and one at the bottom.

Sunday mornings at Shrewsbury were not popular among the smaller boys. The *long-lie*, as it was called, allowing them in theory to enjoy the luxury of an extended rest in bed, was often used for a different purpose. Blankets were pulled from the beds for the traditional tossing; and in addition the young-

sters would sometimes have to kneel at their bedsides, not
to pray (unless for mercy) but to be soundly flogged with
branches taken from the headmaster's disused birches. At this
school the bullying was often topical. 'When Russian *knouting*
was the topic of the day, small boys had to strip in the wash-
room and be *knouted*. When the Assize time came round, the
little fellows went in fear and trembling lest they should be
hanged in imitation.'

Mock-hanging was also one of the terrifying ordeals which
the Marlborough junior had to endure. Here small boys were
suspended in sheets over the banisters. Some victims of this
particular form of terror were so affected by it that they
could hardly speak of Marlborough afterwards without a
shudder. A similar entertainment was carried out at the United
Services College, so the real-life Stalky has told us. From the
top landing the staircase wound round and round, leaving a
sort of well in the middle. 'The condemned criminal—myself
or another—was taken to the top floor and sentence of death
was read out as he stood by the banisters. His eyes were then
blindfolded and a rope with a slip-knot was placed under his
arms. A certain amount of slack was allowed for the first
"drop," to give an uncomfortable jerk. With this preparation
he was launched into space.' One day, unfortunately, a mis-
calculation was made over the amount of slack, and a victim
fell heavily from top to bottom of the well, breaking his
leg. The entertainment had then to be given up.

Perhaps a college with a military bias, as this was, could not
be expected to be any more civilised than the average public
school. Certainly 'Stalky' did not find it so when he first went
there. As the smallest boy in the school he led a life of continued
suspense, caned by the masters, thrashed by the prefects,
and kicked by everyone. 'I must,' he says, 'have been perpetu-
ally black and blue.'

Woolwich Academy, where military cadets were trained
from the age of about twelve, had its own ways of dealing
with fags (known here as 'snookers'). They were compelled

to climb to the top of a cupboard, walk along a narrow ledge with their hands on the ceiling to keep themselves from falling, and then dive through the canopy of the bed some five feet below. Sometimes the 'snooker' would be put into a large basket with another fastened over his head, and rolled about the room. C. L. Tredcroft, who was a cadet in 1848, recorded that in his time he and a companion were ordered to stand on a table one day and shake a basket in which a third unlucky 'snooker' had become jammed. The victim came out upside down on to the floor, and suffered a head injury.

The same officer also recalled that one of the older cadets had been reading the *Arabian Nights*, and decided to bring one of its less agreeable features into the lives of his juniors. He would enter the boy's room with a gang of other old soldiers, and clap his hands; whereupon the others would seize the victim, remove his boots and socks, and turn him upside down and lash his feet to the window bars, so that the leader could bastinado them with a handy rod. The boots and socks would then be put on again and the sufferer propped up at his table in front of his books, after which the bullies proceeded to the room of their next chosen victim.

One is tempted to reflect that this was over a hundred years ago and that barbarities that took place in the rough 1850's could not occur in the present century. But the reflection is distorted. A sailor who entered the Royal Hospital School, Greenwich, during the First World War, has vividly described the miseries he endured at the age of about twelve from boys three or four years older. The dormitories here were enormous, holding over eighty beds, and the bigger boys, like those of the Long Chamber, were lords of all they surveyed, and deliberately made the lives of their juniors unbearable. 'It was a commonplace to see a youngster standing on his bed in his nightshirt, shivering with the cold, holding his boots above his head for an hour after lights out, because a loutish petty-officer boy had so decreed. I have seen, not once but many

The Old Dormitory at Winchester in 1840

times, a big boy smack and punch a little boy's face till it was raw and bleeding.'

It may perhaps be a little depressing to those who believe in 'progressive' education to know that pioneer schools may share the evils of the conventional schools which they despise. Take Bedales, for instance. Here was a school intended to herald a new age, stimulated by the writings of advanced thinkers, and deliberately setting out to break away from the old-established schools. It was to provide an education for the children of parents bold enough to consider reason rather than custom. Bliss was it in that dawn of 1893 to be alive.

Bliss for the founders and parents, perhaps, but not for the smaller boys. The school might be the New Jerusalem in intention, but it was the old Adam who inhabited it. Self-discipline among the boys was the rule, with no repressive supervision by the staff. In theory this should have brought an atmosphere of sweetness and light into school life; in practice it meant simply that the older boys did as they pleased with the younger ones, just as in the bad old days of the Long Chamber at Eton.

'My first year,' wrote E. L. Grant Watson, one of the early pupils, 'contained much acute misery, and even the holidays were clouded . . . When the time came for going back, I was ill with nervousness.' His particular dread was the changing-room, which the small boys (Watson was ten) had to share with the big ones, and were ruthlessly smacked about in the process.

One of the favourite changing-room sports was to fling an unpopular boy into one of the baths. 'Then all the small boys who could be caught were seized and thrown in on top of him, and the big boys would jump on top, shout and sing songs and hit at any portion of the struggling mass with the heels of their slippers,' and also turn on the hot water. It was often a really terrifying ordeal, both for the boy underneath and for the small boys in the middle of the sandwich.

On the whole, there has been little to choose between public schools, military or naval colleges, and private schools. Young Jesse Pearce, at the Greenwich naval school in 1917 'cried for a whole week, off and on, after my return from holidays—and so did a lot of other little boys, with good reason.' A few years earlier Richard Norton, later Lord Grantley, 'with my youthful nerves tormented by the ceaseless bullying and my eyes always red from crying' was imploring his father to take him away from Wellington, where a big lout of seventeen, among other things, forced him to spend

A Bully Defeated

every night of his first term on top of a hot-water cistern instead of in his bed. At Sir Osbert Sitwell's private school, about the same period, at an end-of-term ceremony known as Pay-Day, four or five bigger boys would seize a smaller boy as he emerged into the playground, drag him into a quiet corner, and punch him deliberately in the face, and the victim 'would slink back to school with two black eyes, and a bleeding nose, and sometimes with a tooth or two missing.' (But afterwards there was a school concert and 'Auld Lang Syne.')

Sir Hugh Walpole at a preparatory school in Marlow had two years of 'sheer, stark, unblinking Terror.' Every night at bedtime the bigger boys held a 'Circus' at which their juniors were made to perform. They had to fight one another, and jump from the top of the school lockers to the floor—a feat which filled short-sighted Walpole with dread. Worse still was being roasted in front of the fire, or compelled to swing slowly round on the gas bracket suspended from the ceiling. Worst of all his experiences was being forced to strip naked and stand on a bench while the gang loudly sneered at his body and ended by sticking pins and pen-nibs into it.

It is, of course, easy for the slippered adult in a cosy arm-chair to laugh off these things as harmless fun. But for even the normal child they are neither funny nor harmless: to the sensitive child they are the long-continued agony that Walpole has described. 'Worse than the hour itself was the anticipation of the hour. First thought on waking was that 8.30 p.m. was far away. Then, slowly through the day, it grew ever closer and closer until by tea-time tears of anticipatory fear would fall into one's cup and salten one's hunk of bread . . . One month at Marlow was enough to make me sycophantic, dirty in body and mind, a prey to every conceivable terror, so that the banging of a door or the dropping of a book sent my heart into my cranium.'

Many defenders of boarding-school education assume that

boarding-houses are, and have always been, an essential part of the public school system. This is not so. The boarding element in public school life is largely accidental.

The first great public schools, Winchester and Eton, were boarding-schools not because a communal existence away from home was felt to be a desirable preparation for the normal young gentleman's life, but precisely because they were *not* intended for normal young gentlemen. The specific purpose of these Colleges was to supply the universities with a type of person who would in due course become almost a kind of monk, cut off from the everyday world. 'Paid for from start to finish from College funds,' as a Winchester historian puts it, 'and provided for life with a predestined and celibate career, the Scholars were to look to the College for their home and their centre. Like Plato's Guardians, they were to be taken as children from home and from all private affections and dedicated and trained to the service of God in Church and State.'

In addition to these cloistered celibates, the masters were permitted to take just a few other pupils, fee-payers, sons of influential persons who wished their children to be well grounded in the classics. These few boys did not stay either in college or in boarding-houses, but lived in private houses in the town. They were day boys, living away from their parents because there was no good school nearer home, and because these were days when a distance of a few miles between one town and another separated them as effectively as the English Channel.

A few ancient schools, such as Westminster and King's School, Canterbury, were developments from pre-Reformation monastic or cathedral schools. Almost all of the other older public schools were really town grammar schools, intended primarily for local boys, but receiving a few fee-payers from a distance because, again, well-to-do parents wanted their sons to have a good education and there was no convenient school within reach of home in days before steam and petrol had caused England to shrink. These fee-payers sometimes boarded with the master or his usher, sometimes in private houses, but in neither case were bed and board regarded as part of the process of education.

The numbers of fee-payers at certain schools tended to increase as the years passed, partly because the country's population was growing, partly because, as the reputation of a particular master spread, more and more parents wished their children to have the benefit of his tuition. Schoolmasters naturally encouraged the tendency, which considerably increased their salaries. Local persons boarding a pupil or two in a house near the school also found it profitable to invite others, and parents found it less trouble to send their children to such boarding-houses than to search for separate private accommodation. Thus a system of boarding-houses outside the school grew up. As time went on, masters deemed it both desirable and profitable to take over such houses themselves, the original owners, often elderly dames, having no qualifications whatever for looking after boys. Hence the public school, by the middle of the nineteenth century, had accidentally become mainly or exclusively a boarding-school. New public schools, several of which were founded during the second part of the century, tended to imitate this boarding element in one form or another, and hence the accident became the rule.

This is not the place to discuss at length the merits and defects of boarding-school education. There are obvious benefits that a boy may receive from living in a comparatively closed community, provided he is lucky in his fellows and rulers. But it remains true that a boy, especially a young boy, who is largely cut off from the day-to-day contact with a good home and decent parents loses far more than he gains. Even where the boy is reasonably successful and fairly happy at school the loss is serious, and the practice not really justifiable. 'A school house,' said C. H. P. Mayo, himself a popular Harrow master and a conventional defender of the boarding system, 'is, when you come to think of it, an anomaly, a collection of boys sent away from home at their most impressionable age to be educated by strangers.' That is a far stronger condemnation of the system than he himself realised.

Where a boy is not really happy (and this used to be, and perhaps still is, more often than parents ever allowed themselves to believe) existence in a boarding-school can be a disaster. 'I curse the time as I look back on it,' wrote Lowes Dickinson, who was at Charterhouse. 'Cut off from home life, and they from me, without a root that really sprang from myself, yet tormented by external ties of mere superstition, was there ever a sadder, drearier, more hopeless entry upon life?' Sir Osbert Sitwell, writing of his preparatory school, reminds the reader of 'the continuity of the wretchedness . . . Being a boarding-school this establishment offered a horrible isolation from every warm current of life.'

'I would gladly send a son to a good school by day,' said Southey, 'but rather than board him at the best I would, at whatever inconvenience, educate him myself.'

'We have no hesitation,' asserted Sydney Smith, writing in the *Edinburgh Review*, 'in saying that that education seems to us to be the best which mingles a domestic with a school life.'

A long time has passed since these opinions were expressed, and conditions have greatly changed in boarding-schools, in most respects for the better. But it remains true that, apart from exceptional circumstances, there is no real justification for the artificial world of the boarding-school. It is a monstrous, though unrealised, hypocrisy for parsons and politicians to preach the importance of the home and the family, and then to pack their own children off to be brought up by strangers.

'Home education in conjunction with day schools is the rule all over the civilised world,' so Oscar Browning, himself a distinguished Eton master, declared. 'Home education educates the family as well as the children.'

'The boy at boarding-school,' wrote a distinguished author who had experienced both types of school, 'being away from home eight or nine months in the year, often does not have the slightest idea what his parents are really like.' He himself found his day grammar school a welcome relief from the strained atmosphere of his motherless home; yet he recognised that this home life, unsatisfactory as it was in many ways, was a necessary part of his experience.

That, after all, is the common sense of the matter. So long as the home remains an integral part of English society, we should all learn to know what home means (for better or for worse), and the only way to do this is to live in one.

CHAPTER FOUR

UP, THE REBELS!

W E do not usually associate schools with movements such as the French Revolution and the Declaration of Rights. But there is—or was—a kinship. The spirit which found expression in France in the storming of the Bastille and in America in the Boston Riots was equally present in the hearts of English public schoolboys, and at the same period in history. The latter part of the eighteenth century saw outbreaks of revolt at nearly all of those public schools which regarded themselves as Great. Indeed, one might almost say that one of the distinctions between a major and a minor public school is that the former has at least one rebellion to its discredit.

There are few records of revolt at any school before the time of Wilkes and Rousseau. It may be that real politics played too big a part in a school's life to allow domestic matters to worry either pupils or masters unduly. As often as not the master himself was on the run because his political views did not coincide with those of the King or State. For instance, Lancelot Osbaldeston, headmaster of Westminster, was sentenced by the Star Chamber to be nailed by the ear to a pillory in Dean's Yard because he had once made an injudicious reference to Archbishop Laud. In the same troubled period Alexander Gill, junior, of St Paul's was in difficulties with the same autocratic body, being sentenced to lose one ear in London, the other at Oxford, and to pay a fine of £200 into the bargain. John Biddle of the Crypt Grammar School, Gloucester, was imprisoned for six months, had a book burnt by the common hangman, and died from the effects of his incarceration. Dugard of Merchant Taylors was sacked, committed to Newgate, restored by the intercession of Milton, and dismissed again at the Restoration.

With outside politics entering the school so excitingly, pupils no doubt felt that to revolt over such trifles as the flogging of a monitor or the cancellation of an accustomed privilege would be something of an anti-climax.

The nearest approach to rebellion recorded in this period is the old custom of 'barring-out,' which is almost literally playing at revolt. As the great festivals of Christmas and Easter drew near, often though not inevitably bringing with them a time of vacation, the scholars used to take possession of the single schoolroom, barricade the doors, and shout defiance from the windows. It seems a practice full of sound and fury, and, says Dr Johnson, 'if tradition may be credited, the master often struggled hard to force or surprise the garrison.' None the less, the struggles, if the written word may be credited, cannot often have been serious. Charles Hoole, a wise and capable schoolmaster of the seventeenth century, accepts 'barring-out' as a custom worth keeping (with due safeguards); and in one school it is actually demanded by statute. 'According to the old custom,' says this Elizabethan edict, 'they shall bar and keep forth of the school the schoolmaster, in such sort as other scholars do in the great schools.'

Even this mock form of mutiny had died out by the end of the seventeenth century, and for a while nothing more serious took its place. There is mention in one or two records of 'a state of anarchy' at Eton in 1729, but there is no evidence that it amounted to much.

Forty years on a new spirit was abroad. John Wilkes had triumphantly resisted illegal arrest; the American colonies had successfully resisted the Stamp Act. It is rather improbable that public schoolboys had made a close study of those contemporary milestones of history, but it is certain that the growing spirit of mass resistance to real or supposed tyranny had seeped into the schools. At all events, the year 1768 saw the flag of revolt hoisted over the distant spires and antique towers of Eton.

The behaviour of the school authorities seems in this case, as in several others, to have been quite remarkably inept. The Sixth Form Praepostors, or Prefects, had the power to punish, for breaking bounds, any lower form boys they might meet outside the College. This would seem to suggest that the prefects themselves were entitled to a wider liberty than their juniors; and when, in the autumn of 1768, the assistant masters claimed the right to deal with prefects as the prefects dealt with lower boys, the claim was vigorously opposed. The headmaster, Dr John Foster, attempted ineffectively to smooth the trouble over.

A modern headmaster would be in a happier position to act as peacemaker, for his authority as ruler of the school is now unquestioned. Unfortunately for Foster, an Eton headmaster's rights were vaguer in the eighteenth century than they are today, and unfortunately for the praepostors, their rights were vaguer still. Dr Foster adopted the view that assistant masters must be supported, right or wrong, and when one of them brought a praepostor before the headmaster for punishment, Foster flogged him in spite of a threat by his colleagues to resign their duties.

A wiser and stronger Head than Foster, having proved his readiness to support his staff even at the expense of justice, might now have been determined to meet the ex-praepostors half way, whether the masters liked it or not. Foster, on the other hand, refused to meet the boys' claims at all, even though they advanced the reasonable proposition that they should be punished if they were found in taverns or other improper places but not merely for being outside the college precincts. Unable to secure any sort of compromise, they refused to take part in the forthcoming Declamation ceremony, and were threatened with expulsion. Almost the whole of the senior school supported the praepostors. A council of war was held in the playing-fields. Subsequently an army of 160 boys marched deliberately from the school. Rebellion was afoot.

It was a very genteel revolt. Having no particular precedent to follow, the leaders seem to have been rather at a loss how to proceed. The rebels marched up river to Maidenhead, probably in good order, and stayed the night at an inn. Then, following the precedent of the Grand Old Duke of York, they marched back again.

So polite a demonstration could not achieve anything. The tyrants had suffered no discomfort and the school no damage, unless we accept a doubtful tradition that the boys threw all their books into the Thames. (Their parents paid for books, in any case.) An offer to capitulate on condition that all should be treated alike was rejected. Foster insisted on unconditional surrender.

He won the day. Many of the rebels, perhaps all, were flogged, including some who had tried to enlist parental support. On a short-term view Foster had conquered by firmness. But firm opposition to moderate complaint may be weakness in diguise. The way to good government in school is to gain the support of the older boys, as Arnold was later to prove beyond all question. Foster had really missed his chance, and both he and the school suffered. In eight years the numbers were reduced by more than half, and he himself gave up the struggle, broken in health, at the early age of 41.

Eton's precedent was soon followed. Two years later Winchester copied the act, but without the moderation; and it may not be without significance that the ringleader was a boy previously expelled from Eton. The landlord of the White Hart inn had offended a bunch of Winchester lads, who were boozing in his house, by telling them to stop drinking and go home. The next evening they decided to go and break his windows, just to show him that Winchester boys could not be trifled with. A party thereupon set out, armed with cudgels and pistols.

The headmaster, Dr Warton, discovered what was happening

and endeavoured to prevent any further trouble by locking up the remaining Commoners* in their building. They forced the doors in spite of him; and the Collegers, also locked up, created such a disturbance that they too had to be released to join the fray. A townsman was shot in the leg, the landlord having gathered some friends to help him. Having tasted blood, the boys sallied forth again the next evening, and the ensuing fight was so violent that magistrates had to be called to read the Riot Act.

Disaffection had spread to Harrow by the following year, when there was a minor mutiny over the appointment of a new headmaster; and in 1774 Dr Warton of Winchester was in trouble again with a new group of rowdies.

At an impromptu dramatic performance in the Common Hall, one of the boys took off the housekeeper, an old woman with a humped back. The victim saw the caricature, and complained to the Commoners' Tutor, a Mr Huntingford (a name worth remembering). Rather unwisely, he ordered them all off to bed. They refused to go. Dr Warton now came into the hall. He ordered a boy to burn a wig and mask which he saw, saying that he would have no masquerades in his school. When he went to leave the hall all the boys hissed him.

'So, gentlemen! Are you all metamorphosed into serpents?' cried the headmaster. They were indeed, drowning with even greater hisses his subsequent attempts to address them. The next day the forty or so boys concerned, failing to secure the dismissal of the unpopular Mr Huntingford, marched away from the school.

This had already at Eton been proved an ineffective method of rebellion. The master holds all the cards in a game of patience. He has but to wait, and the parents will do the rest. The runaways suffered a good deal of hardship on the homeward journey, and in the end had to submit or be expelled.

A more serious affair developed at Eton in 1783, the assistant

---

* Seventy boys received free education, as the founder had laid down, and were known as Collegers. All other boys were Commoners.

masters being once again indirectly responsible. They could not get on with the headmaster, Dr Davies, who, they complained to the Provost, behaved towards them in an ungentlemanly way. While acrimonious negotiations were going on they withdrew their services, leaving Dr Davies to cope with the Upper School alone. Some of the scholars, it seems, shared the masters' dislike of the Head, and thought the present occasion provided an opportunity too good to be missed. A list of grievances and requests was drawn up by ten of the Oppidans,* supported by the lower forms though not by all the seniors. The headmaster refused to relax his rule whether his assistants were present or not. A violent revolt followed. Dr Davies was driven from the Upper School, and had to escape for safety by a back door to the Provost's Lodge. The rebels broke all the windows in the School, after which, growing bolder, they entered the headmaster's own rooms, smashed his furniture, and destroyed his papers. The flogging-block, over which offenders were stretched when they were flogged, was hacked and burnt with knives and red-hot pokers, and chunks of it were taken away as trophies.

By this time it was becoming evident to the assistant masters that if they were too precise in sticking to terms of agreement there would be no school left for them to return to. They thereupon accepted Dr Davies's peace overtures, and the rebellion petered out. None the less, the boys were sent home for their Christmas holiday almost at once, so the revolt at any rate won them an extension of vacation.

In 1791 all the boys at Westminster School walked out over a disagreement with the headmaster, Dr Vincent. The cause of the dispute was curious. The boys were too busy watching a fight one day in Dean's Yard to bother about lessons; and first one master, then another, and finally Dr Vincent himself went in vain to summon them to school. No one, perhaps not even the boys themselves, could have demurred if the whole school had been punished for disobedience. As

* Equivalent to the Commoners at Winchester.

it was, if the account in a contemporary newspaper is to be credited, the only person Dr Vincent proposed to punish was the head boy, who was not present at the fight. The whole school protested against his flogging, and a general desertion followed. The matter was only settled by the boy himself, a public-spirited young fellow of 19, who consented to read a public apology rather than lessen the headmaster's authority by allowing the rebellion to continue.

There are few headmasters who have met trouble with such dignity as this head boy.

Most of the rebellions we have considered might well have been avoided by a little sense and prudence on the part of the school authorities. This is even truer of the affair at Winchester in 1793 (the year when Louis XVI and Marie Antoinette were dragged to the scaffold), which is known in the annals of the College as the Great Rebellion. In this case the headmaster, the unfortunate Dr Warton, was hardly to blame. The direction of College discipline was mainly in the hands of the Warden, and the Warden at this time was the obnoxious Mr Huntingford who had precipitated trouble when he was the Commoners' Tutor nineteen years before.

This time he began the trouble by refusing to allow Winchester boys to attend the parade of the Bucks Militia, which took place not far from the school. 'If any one individual is peccant, he shall be severely punished; but if numbers are seen, the whole school shall be punished by being refused leave out to dine with their friends.' A boy *was* seen at the parade, reported, and severely punished. At the same time, though only one offender had been seen, the punishment was extended to the whole school: leave the next day was cancelled, just as if the Warden's ban had been generally defied.

The injustice of this action naturally rankled, but the leaders of the school showed a restraint very different from the behaviour of the riotous gang of roaring boys who had swaggered off to break the windows of the White Hart twenty years earlier. A meeting was held that evening, at which it was wisely resolved, 'That we should not proceed to violent measures till every lenient one was tried in vain.' Feeling, none the less, was as strong as if a new Declaration of Independence were being drawn up. The forty-seven seniors pledged themselves to stand together in approaching the Warden, and took a solemn oath to the effect 'that the assembly shall subscribe their names to this paper, and keep their plighted faith, as they will answer for it at the tribunal of Almighty God.' The remaining thirty boys were not allowed to sign the oath, as being too young to understand the implications of it, but they promised their support.

A letter, written in Latin, was then drawn up, respectfully requesting that in future 'you will not punish *all* for the sake of *one*.'

So reasonable a demand expressed in such reasonable terms should hardly have offended a King, yet alone a Warden; but Mr Huntingford did not deign to offer it a reply. After three days of anxious waiting they wrote again, still almost embarrassingly mild in their approach. Relying upon his kindness, they said, they had thought fit to write to him. They trusted that he would no longer keep them in suspense for an answer.

To this tactful follow-up letter the insufferable Warden replied, on the back of their own paper:

'When scholars are so forgetful of their rank and good manners as to insult their Warden by a letter of the most consummate arrogance and extreme petulance, he can give them no other answer than that he shall continue to refuse them every indulgence till they behave with propriety.'

Obviously no satisfaction was to be gained by polite requests to this pompous ass. They must grin and bear his domination unless they were prepared to make a more sensational protest.

Consultations were held and an act of war followed. A group of boys seized some of the College keys. A message was sent to Mr Goddard, the Lower Master (the man responsible for reporting the original offender), advising him not to come to the school that afternoon. He disregarded the message and was received with shouts and hisses. 'Finding some marbles rattling about his ears, he retired,' a schoolboy chronicler remarks succinctly.

A request to the headmaster also to absent himself was softened by a warm and sincere expression of the boys' esteem for him personally. He was sensible enough to regard the message, and went to see the Warden instead. The latter sent for the eighteen prefects to appear before him, but they had previously decided not to obey such a summons, as it would almost certainly be the prelude to a wholesale expulsion.

The boys now had possession of all the keys, and they used them, strategically, to keep the enemy's forces divided. The Warden had sent hastily for four of the College Fellows (who were in a sense his co-governors), obviously intending to devise some drastic action. Realising that no important decision could be taken unless all four Fellows were present, the boys contrived to lock one of the Fellows inside the college and keep the rest outside. Mr Goddard was locked up in the Warden's house, and the passage between this and the masters' lodgings was effectively blocked and patrolled. The Warden was subsequently allowed to go into the town, but found himself locked out of the College precincts when he tried to return.

He was now so baffled that he sent a message to say that all the boys might go home for a holiday, provided that the masters approved. This seemed too much like a trap. They refused the bait, and kept him outside the gates. In despair, he went off to fetch the magistrates.

It seemed likely that force was to be used, so the boys prepared for war. They barricaded the gates, armed themselves with swords and cudgels, and laid in a store of food—in which activity they were unwillingly assisted by a baker and a female butcher whose wares were conveniently within confiscating distance. They then took possession of the tower over the gateway, pulling up stones and loosening slabs from the parapet in order to obtain ammunition, and prepared if necessary to light faggots to drop on the heads of unwise storm troopers. The influence of the French Revolution now became explicit. A Red Cap of Liberty was hoisted, and red caps were worn by as many boys as could find or make them.

Such events could not take place in a country town without receiving publicity. A crowd of two thousand had gathered round the gate by the time one of the magistrates appeared, and some fools even suggested firing at the boys through the openings. They were disappointed if they were expecting a battle to commence, for the magistrates were by no means anxious to storm this particular Bastille. The ambassador was persuasive and friendly. After inducing the Warden and Fellows to grant a general amnesty, he prevailed upon the rebels to hand over the keys. They did so at last, the Warden promising in future not to punish the whole community for the sake of one person, which was the very point they were fighting for. Superficially they had triumphed.

But a Warden's word must not be taken too seriously. Once the school precincts were gained the Warden did not worry himself unduly about the terms he had agreed. Anxious to save his face, he persuaded or coerced a number of parents into temporarily removing their sons unless they apologised. The rest of the forty determined to stand up for liberty and fair play, and accordingly resigned from their places as scholars. This was a tactical error. The Warden promptly accepted the resignations. The boys attempted to withdraw them the following day, but it was too late. The Warden preferred the scandal of wholesale departure of the senior Collegers to the ignominy of defeat. Thus the Great Rebellion in the long run brought as little reward to its determined leaders as rebellions of the weak against the strong usually do.

Rugby, too, had its Great Rebellion, which took place four years after Winchester's, and was no doubt partly inspired by the spirit of 'Liberty, Equality, and Fraternity,' even though red caps were not worn by the insurgents.

The starting-point was a walk taken by the headmaster,

Dr Ingles, a dignified, severe man, whose entry into the Upper Schoolroom produced 'a silence like a chill,' and who was known throughout the school as the Black Tiger. As he approached one of the houses where some of the scholars were boarded he heard sounds of firing. Investigation revealed a boy firing corks at a window. He was asked where he had bought the gunpowder, and gave the name of the seller—a man who kept a general shop where he sold groceries, books, and ironmongery. Tradesmen were strictly forbidden to sell weapons or explosives to the schoolboys, so the cautious shopkeeper had entered the sale of the gunpowder as 'tea.' The headmaster thereupon flogged the boy for lying.

Schoolboys in those days had one inevitable method of arguing with a tradesman. They smashed his windows. The shopkeeper in this case complained, and Dr Ingles insisted that the boys must pay for the repair of the windows. They refused, a deputation of the Sixth and Fifth presenting a round robin, signed by the members of these forms, indicating their objections. The headmaster threatened severe measures. The blood of the Rugbeians was at fever heat. They found some more gunpowder, applied it to the master's door and blew it off its hinges. To this violent argument the headmaster at first seemed to have no answer; and indeed, even in those days, teachers did not normally expect to come under quite such heavy fire.

Absence of retribution went to the heads of the rioters. After first lesson the next day—and it must have been an uneasy lesson on both sides of the schoolroom—the school bell rang out wildly. It was the call to arms. Benches and desks were smashed and dragged out to the Close, and a huge bonfire lit. Even the wainscoting was torn from the walls of the schoolrooms to feed the flames. Windows were smashed, the smaller boys being hoisted on the shoulders of their seniors so that they could penetrate the protective lattice-work with pointed sticks.

Unfortunately for Dr Ingles, most of the masters had left

the building, for it was a Saturday and mainly a holiday. The headmaster found himself virtually alone to deal with the outburst, and for the moment he was powerless. The ringleaders actually threatened him with personal violence, and he had to shut himself up in his house for safety.

Help, however, was at hand. A recruiting party, he recollected, was at the November horse-fair, then being held in the town; and a message was secretly conveyed to the sergeant in charge.

Soldiers and schoolboys in those days were rarely good friends. The sergeant had no hesitation in complying. His troop was reinforced by volunteers consisting of special constables, farmers (with many an old score to pay off against the Tom Browns of the time) and a few returning masters. Confronted by this army, the boys retreated to the Island in the school field, which really was an island, with a moat fifteen feet wide and four or five feet deep. They pulled up the drawbridge, and doubtless expected a siege.

They were less skilled or less fortunate than their Wincastrian counterparts. Though a future general was among their leaders, they allowed themselves to be sadly outgeneralled by a mere recruiting sergeant. While someone in authority was reading the Riot Act in front of the drawn bridge, the sergeant and his men waded through the moat and surprised the garrison in the rear. The rebels had no effective answer to a drawn sword, and capitulated. Another Great Rebellion was over; and once again nothing permanent was achieved. The leaders were expelled or flogged; and Dr Ingles continued his stern rule for a good many years to come.

Early in the new century, Harrow was again in revolt, as usual over the appointment of a new headmaster. The popular Joseph Drury was succeeded by Rev. George Butler instead of the retiring Head's brother, Mark. Feelings in those times were strong, and were strongly expressed. One of the monitors who favoured Drury was Byron; and his opposition to the new headmaster was shown not only by his tearing down the gratings which protected the hall windows but also (according to one story) by his carrying a loaded pistol with which to make his dislike of Butlerism even more explicit. Fortunately it does not seem to have been used.

Open rebellion is said to have lasted three days, during which a train of gunpowder was laid in a passage which the Doctor was known to use at night. The train was fired, without effect; and the perpetrators were never discovered. There seems to have been a plan for setting the schoolroom on fire; and on this occasion Byron, according to his own subsequent story, acted in the unusual role of a restraining influence, pointing out to his fellows the names of their fathers and grandfathers on the walls which were being threatened with arson.

Three years later Dr Butler was again having trouble with the Harrow monitors, the matter in dispute being their complete independence to cane their juniors at will. Ironically enough, the school supported the monitors. There was a general strike, and seven monitors were ultimately expelled.

This was the era of the great Eton rebellions; partly, no doubt, because it was also the era of the renowned Dr Keate. This notorious headmaster inaugurated a Reign of Terror which provoked the bolder spirits to mingle defiance with their dread. Keate ruled from 1809 to 1834, and in that period there were no fewer than three major rebellions. On the surface the master seems to have been in the right on each occasion; but Keate, with his vicious snarl and furious manner (like an angry bullfrog, it was said) was just the man to turn right into wrong.

As under-master he was already known and hated; and he met with opposition from the first. The keyhole of his door was blocked up with a bullet, forcing him to enter the school by the further door and walk the length of the schoolroom to shouts of 'Boo, boo!' On reaching the platform on which his desk stood, enclosed all round like an old-fashioned church pew, he found the door screwed fast. He tried the door on the other side: that was fastened too. Not to be beaten he vaulted over, to the shouts and mutinous cheers of the boys.

'I'll make some of you suffer for this!' he snarled; but the offenders were never discovered.

With this spirit already simmering in the school, it was almost inevitable that major outbreaks should occasionally occur. That they did not burst out more often was due to Keate's own spirit, for whatever his faults, he did not lack the courage to face opposition.

A year after his accession he was given his first opportunity as a riot-breaker. Boys in the lower part of the Fifth Form had got into the bad habit of hanging about outside the Chapel door until the masters arrived, and then rushing to their places. Some headmasters would have achieved a reform by a timely remonstrance; but Keate's methods were different. He cut in half the two hours of freedom, from four to six, which the boys were accustomed to enjoy on whole holidays, thus punishing guilty and innocent alike. All lower Fifth boys were ordered to answer to their names at five in future. On this occasion almost the whole group deliberately ignored the roll-call.

Keate did not hesitate to administer the usual punishment of 'six cuts with a birch rod' to every absentee, but the spirit of mutiny was still abroad. By the time the first twenty victims had been dealt with the rest were shouting abuse and even throwing rotten eggs at the Master. Eventually, indeed, the whole eighty boys were compelled to submit to the flogging, subdued by the calling in of the Assistant Masters and the threat of immediate expulsion. Even so, the Doctor's victory was hardly final. The custom of loitering in the ante-chapel was revived by some forty of the boys after the holidays, and Keate's angry rebukes met with retaliatory shouts as the boys went in and out of Chapel. On one occasion, moreover, Keate was bolted out before the service.

Nine years later mischief on a larger scale was afoot. The winter lock-up hour for boarding-houses was advanced from six o'clock to five. The reason, or at any rate the ostensible reason, for shortening the pupils' freedom was the long-continued prevalence of hunting, shooting, and tandem-driving. In days when pupils' leisure time was very much their own, these (as we should think) unschoolboy-like activities were commonly engaged in at more than one school. If not officially tolerated, they were at any rate often winked at by authority. Keate's belated decision to stamp them out was fully justified in itself; but his manner of doing it combined, as usual, the maximum of provocation with the minimum of tact.

The result was perhaps to be expected. 'The whole School [we are told] was in ferment for several days. Detonating balls (a type of miniature hand-grenade), bought at Windsor Fair, were thrown about during lessons, the windows of a master's house were smashed, and part of the wall of Long Walk was thrown down.'

One of the chief tandem-drivers, though only a lower boy, was privately expelled. But the news leaked out, and when Keate entered the schoolroom next day he was greeted with furious shouts of, 'Where's Marriot?' Unable to make himself heard, he left his desk and went out of the room, followed by a volley of bad eggs. His retreat was only strategic; and he returned soon afterwards with several of the assistant masters, instructing them to seize anyone who spoke. Order was restored superficially; but there was no true spirit of discipline behind it. A sense of unfairness was left, as always with Keate.

Two days later there was a sequel. The headmaster's great desk at the end of Upper School was found smashed to pieces. Keate took no notice, standing on the bare platform throughout eleven o'clock school as though the shattered desk had never existed. But he was not the man to turn his back on such an outrage; and chance came to his assistance. His servant, it happened, had seen a young Colleger leaving Upper School at an unusual hour the previous day. The child was ruthlessly examined by a Council of masters, and, though innocent enough himself, was driven by fear to confess that he had accidentally seen the culprits, and to give their names. They were all high in the Fifth Form; two of them were Collegers (and therefore subject to the discipline of the Provost), and four Oppidans, whom the headmaster could deal with directly. They were all solemnly expelled at a meeting of the whole school, and when Keate provocatively snarled that perhaps this would teach the rest of the school to behave better in future, another boy was heard by a master to murmur 'Never!' —so he was expelled too, though he was a boy of excellent character.

Even now the trouble was not over. Placards were found in prominent places about the College, inscribed 'Down with Keate!' 'No five o'clock absence,' '*Floreat seditio*,' and similar encouragements to revolt. One youngster of thirteen felt so strongly against Keate's apparent injustices, and was so determined not to submit to them, that his father, a judge, had to remove him. By the end of another week or so, Keate proudly claimed that the rebellion had been crushed, and that the boys were now 'as quiet as lambs.' Yet after all the tumult and the shouting that he had provoked, his achievement in the end was insignificant. Tandem-driving still continued during Keate's reign, and was not abolished until a different spirit had been brought into the school by headmasters using a different approach.

Before this new era, however, Eton had experienced one more Great Rebellion. Keate was still on the throne, though close to retirement. As usual, the direct cause was a curtailment of privilege, in the form of enforced attendance at extra 'absences' or roll-calls.

A popular boy was removed from the school for some offence, unjustly as it seemed to some of his fellows. When the next absence was called, many of the boys shouted and booed at the obvious omission of his name. Keate, no more inclined to conciliate now than he was twenty years earlier, ordered for the main offenders, the Lower Fifth, three extra holiday roll-calls until further notice. The one which stung particularly was that at 8 p.m., for some of the Lower Fifth belonged to the boat-crews who were in the habit of supping at Surly Hall, up river, on certain Saturday evenings in the summer term. A week went by and Keate showed no sign of relenting, so the wet bobs persuaded the rest of the Lower Fifth to join in a revolt. Only two boys out of about eighty were present to answer their names on the following Saturday.

During his twenty-three years of headmastership Keate had learnt little in the art of bringing out the best in boys; but he had at least learnt something in the technique of handling rebellion. The unruly scene which had occurred in 1810, when the mass flogging was accompanied by shouts and egg-throwing, was skilfully avoided, thanks partly to his own generalship but even more to the tactful co-operation of his assistant masters. The rebels were attacked at night, when they did not expect it; and their forces were skilfully split into insignificant groups. True, an attempt to secure co-ordination was made by the insurgents of one House, who shouted from the windows, 'Don't submit to be flogged! We haven't been flogged!' But courage is not at its height in the silent hours of night, without the actual presence of a crowd of fellow-resisters. Alone, or almost alone, in Keate's presence, all of the rebels but a handful meekly submitted to the rod.

The scene of this unhappy night has been graphically portrayed by one of the victims.

'No sooner were we safe in our tutors' and dames' houses than Keate summoned a council of war. I was comfortably asleep at a quarter past eleven when a light appeared in my room, and Pickering (a great favourite with us, his first pupils) stood before me in cap and gown.

' "B——," he said, "I have come to ask you whether you intentionally stayed away from the absence this evening?"

' "Why, yes, sir, I think I did."

' "Then perhaps you will have no objection to come with me and tell Dr Keate so?"

' "Oh!" I answered, not exactly seeing the necessity for such a step at that most unseasonable hour. "I will tomorrow; I am sure he will believe you, if you tell him."

' "I had much rather that he heard it from *you*: indeed you will greatly oblige me if you will come with me at once and explain the matter to him."

'Such an appeal was unanswerable and I promised to be ready in a few minutes. He was waiting in the Hall, where I found four fellow-delinquents already assembled. Headed by him we sallied out towards the school-yard instead of Keate's house. A single lamp was over Keate's chambers, and by its light we could see a group of figures at each pillar of the row of arches. My tutor led us to a vacant one and there was a dead silence. We could see by the reflection that there were lights in the room above. Presently a clattering of feet, and down came half a dozen fellows. We could not see who they were, or speak to them, and they turned under the archway and vanished. This was repeated more than once, successive groups vacating their post and ascending the stairs. The "explanation" did not seem to take up much time . . .

'However, our turn soon came. My tutor went forward to the door, and returned with a most polite, "Now, if you please," ushered us to the foot of the stairs, and went off in search of further victims.

'A Colleger with about a dozen long rods was handing them fresh to Keate, who with a very dignified air cast the used ones behind him.

'Looking at his list, Keate called my name. "B——, I did not expect this of you—kneel down." Practice makes perfect; and perhaps knowing that there was plenty of work before him he was unusually expeditious.

'An hour later the work of castigation was still in progress. A few stood out, but finding themselves in a minority, sub-

mitted with good grace, and so our incipient rebellion came
to an ignominious end.'

This was not only the last of the Eton rebellions; it was almost
the last major revolt in any public school. It was four years
since Arnold had begun with his new broom at Rugby, and
already antagonism between schoolmasters and Seniors (by
no means universal at any time) was growing rarer.
Without the leadership of the older boys, rebellion on a
large scale became impossible. Here and there it gave
an occasional flicker, and on one occasion, at Marlborough,
it became a violent conflagration. After that the flames died
down.

Strangely enough, it was at Rugby that one of the last
outbreaks occurred, in spite of Arnold's overwhelming influence. Or perhaps, after all, it was because of Arnold's influence,
for his successor, afterwards Archbishop Tait, had more to
live up to than he could well manage. Among his other
qualities Arnold had always contrived to leave his pupils,
upper and lower, with the feeling that they were being
fairly dealt with. His punishments were sometimes severe,
but they were explicit. Tait's failure to follow this sound
practice landed him in trouble soon after his accession to the
headship.

During calling-over one morning, after the upper forms
had left, the headmaster announced that in consequence of
some disgraceful conduct, which he did not specify, on the
part of certain boys, whom he did not and perhaps could not
name, the whole town would be out of bounds to the Lower
School, including the Upper Fourth.

Dismay and indignation swamped the boys, most of whom
were doubtless innocent. Angry hisses spread all over Big
School. The headmaster showed firmness in dealing with this
indiscipline, and sent for birches and the flogging-block.
All the boys who had hissed were told to go to one side of the
room. About eighty of one hundred and forty did so. Keate

would have flogged the lot, which would at least have been consistent. Tait picked out every tenth boy to kneel over the block, thereby adding unfairness to injustice.

The flogging passed off without further rioting, but a school accustomed to Arnold's methods could not tolerate such a headmasterly backsliding. Tait was soon made aware of his failure. Not only were the eight victims treated as popular heroes by their comrades. The prefects and the staff also made clear their disapproval of the headmaster's approach. At least a hundred boys deliberately broke bounds that evening. The prefects cheerfully waved them on, and a master who ran into one of the rebels, and who might have given him five hundred lines of Virgil, solemnly ordered him to write out *one* line.

Tait at least had the sense to learn from his mistakes. He let the matter drop, and this minor rebellion was thus one of the few to succeed.

Even more successful was the final outbreak in public school history, which occurred rather less than ten years after the affair at Rugby.

Marlborough at this time was, to be exact, scarcely a public school. It had been opened for barely eight years, and its large numbers, about four hundred, were due entirely to the fact that it was absurdly cheap. The organisers of the enterprise knew as little about running schools as the headmaster and staff knew about teaching in them. The education given was about as bad as any in England, and the conditions under which the boys were brought up had most of the disadvantages of the older public schools at their worst without the mitigation of a long tradition and a venerable building.

Keate's floggings were sadistic and indefensible, but Keate was at least a character in his own right—feared, hated, and sometimes defied, but withal a personality. The masters at Marlborough flogged and caned as furiously as Keate, but without even the redeeming feature of colourfulness. They were almost universally hated.

The headmaster—who was 'a Mr Wilkinson, a clergyman,' as if in mockery of Wordsworth—aroused anger and resentment, where fear and dislike already existed, by unjustly punishing the many for the sins of the few. Tait had learned the folly of this, being well taught by his subordinates; but Wilkinson's staff were even stupider than himself and his contact with his senior boys was remote. So the headmaster's only remedy for angry discontent was to increase it by giving fresh cause for it. If the removal of a general privilege produced resentment, Mr Wilkinson had no way of dealing with the situation except by the removal of another general privilege, and then another. This is the worst of all ways of attacking indiscipline. In due course every boy in the school felt that since he was already being heavily punished whether guilty or not he might just as well have a fling for his money. An explosion was all but inevitable.

The moment came, appropriately enough, round about Guy Fawkes time.

The immediate cause was the behaviour of Peviar, the school porter, a most unpopular character who used to act as a spy on the boys out of school, jotting down in an officious notebook any evidence he could get regarding bad language or other schoolboy misdemeanours. Naturally the boys detested him, and showed their feelings by throwing stones at his lodge by the school gate. One evening late in October, 1851, he had annoyed them even more than usual. An attack in force was made on his lodge. This was, of course, reported to the headmaster, who forthwith confined the whole school to the schoolroom.

The result was a spontaneous revolt. 'For the next four days the boys did practically no work, broke out in the evenings where possible, smashed windows freely, and pelted and hissed every master who attempted to keep order.' At the end of this time the headmaster tried different tactics. He gave up the attempt to punish the whole school, found a scapegoat, who was perhaps one of the leaders, and expelled him.

The boys were by no means appeased. The 5th of November, moreover, was close at hand. It was then a time of licence all over the country; to a crowd of schoolboys in strongly rebellious mood it was an invitation to riot. The purchase of fireworks was emphatically forbidden, but this was no barrier to resentful and ingenious boys. A subscription list was opened, a treasurer appointed—or perhaps self-appointed—and a large stock of explosives laid in, including eighty dozen squibs, crackers, 'and heavier artillery.'

The ringleaders made it known to the school that there would be a grand entertainment in the Court that evening. It began punctually at five o'clock with a rocket shooting upwards; and thereafter squibs and crackers were exploding all the evening, especially when a master made his appearance and tried to stop the show. 'Not content with this,' says an eye-witness, 'the boys carried them into school, let them off under the desks, tossed them into the fires, hissing, stamping, and shouting down the futile attempts of the form-masters to quell the disorder. All that night the row continued, and the echoing corridors of B House rang with the continual detonations. The whole College for the next two days reeked of gunpowder.'

Despairing of punishing the whole school again Mr Wilkinson continued the policy of seeking scapegoats and ringleaders. Five victims were chosen, among them the fireworks treasurer, a most popular prefect. His dismissal became the occasion of a tremendous demonstration. The whole school marched with his carriage towards the town, shouting and cheering.

By the time they were on the return journey they were ready for anything. Their first victim was a miller, one of the boys' constant enemies. He was riding his donkey towards them, and to do him justice, he had the sense to recognise that there was danger in the air. He turned his animal round and prepared for flight, 'bending his body almost double [says one of the older boys], sticking his heels into his donkey's sides, and working his arms and legs as the winner of the Derby does when he approaches the winning-post.' The miller, however, never reached his winning-post. His over-weighted donkey was caught and its rider dragged from his seat and rolled over and over in the gutter.

When the angry mob of boys reached the school gates again, the hated Peviar was unwise enough or unlucky enough to ring the bell to summon them to school. He fled to his lodge with stones whistling round his ears. Some of the boys rushed outside the headmaster's own room, groaning, booing, and hissing, and smashed every pane of glass in the window. Again the bell summoned them into school. All the masters, whose angry canes normally chilled the hearts of their wretched pupils, came forward to frighten their classes into discipline. The attempt was a disaster. The boys booed and groaned, slammed their desks, and stamped their feet. Authority was defeated.

Chaos continued to reign for nearly a week. The schoolroom was in almost continuous uproar. Fireworks were still produced, and were even tossed into the fires beside which masters were actually standing. A bottle filled with gunpowder exploded like a bomb behind the headmaster's back when he stood before the great fireplace in an attempt to awe the school into submission. Windows were smashed and desks broken up. The wooden wings of the racket court were set on fire.

At the end of the week Mr Wilkinson virtually capitulated before the rebels. Calling the school together he requested them to state their grievances. They demanded back all the privileges which they had lost since the school first opened, particularly those connected with outside liberty. The headmaster agreed to this, on condition that £10 was subscribed towards the cost of the damage, and an apology offered.

For a time the truce held. But appeasement, though in this case it was almost inevitable, is a dangerous way of pacifying rebels, especially when the appeasers are normally tyrants. Many of the boys would now have been content to let matters rest, but there were some who were not. Early in December there was another outbreak against the staff. A group of boys went round the great schoolroom breaking open the masters' desks, smashing them to splinters and putting their contents, including registers and punishment books, on the resulting bonfire. A manuscript edition of Sophocles which the headmaster had long been preparing was added to the flames. The masters' own rooms were even raided to supply fuel for the bonfire, while Chapel was in progress, and an attempt was made to set fire to the whole school.

Mr Wilkinson was in despair. He sent for one of the senior boys, saying he did not know who to trust, and was anxious to know whether skeleton keys were being used. The boy could not help him, and was indeed, quite shocked to discover the fearful headmaster, hitherto looked upon as almost an angry god, as much in distress as an ordinary mortal.

Once again, in due course, the trouble was settled. This time, because only a section of the school was in sympathy with the trouble-makers, severity and not capitulation was tried. Batches of boys were flogged; five ringleaders were discovered and expelled. But in the end it was the school that expelled the headmaster. Mr Wilkinson was a beaten and broken man. He resigned the following term and withdrew to the peace of a country church, leaving behind him something like the ruins of a school.

That was the last of the great school rebellions.

Of course, there have been lesser outbreaks. Such was the storming of Windsor by Eton boys in 1874. A political election was being held, and the headmaster, Dr Hornby, put the town out of bounds. A body of two or three hundred boys, bent on challenging the ban, found their way over Windsor Bridge barred by a group of masters. Putting their heads down the boys charged, and were a good deal more successful than the Tuscans against Horatius on a similar occasion.

There were exciting chases during the rest of the evening,

the Windsor tradesmen and other residents showing themselves sportingly ready to help the hunted. Remarkably few captures were made. The unlucky few were duly flogged; but no fuss was made about the school's general defiance of a definite order, Dr Hornby, most easy-going of headmasters, philosophically accepting that he had lost the battle, and adopting the view that the less said about it the better. Opposition to so genteel a ruler can hardly rank as rebellion.

At least a couple of unseemly disturbances have occurred, strangely enough, over that most seemly monarch, Queen Victoria. At the very end of the century a group of boys at Shrewsbury were so disgusted that a half-holiday was not granted in honour of her birthday that, instead of going to lessons, they persuaded most of the school to assemble on the roof and sing patriotic songs, including 'God Save the Queen,' while the masters in caps and gowns glared up helplessly below. This was cheerful defiance rather than rebellion; and it is a mark of the difference that the offenders were passed over to the Sixth Form for punishment.

The other revolt, which occurred at the Leys School at about the same period, was a rather more serious business. At this school the granting of a holiday on the Queen's birthday was a custom which a new headmaster decided to abolish.

The abolition was received with angry opposition. Boys assembled in the early morning outside the headmaster's private house, bawling his name and daring him to come out. A prefect who came to parley with the royalists was assaulted. A master who attempted to intimidate them was lucky to escape without injury.

In despair, the Head called in the police, and a small force of constabulary cavalry galloped down Trumpington Street and into the school grounds. But the rebels, learning of their approach, had strategically mustered on the playing-fields, armed with lacrosse sticks and various types of ball ammunition. This was aimed at the legs and flanks of the horses, and it was the police and not the pupils that eventually dispersed.

Hunger was a more formidable enemy. In the end it drove the rebels to capitulate; and many floggings and some expulsions ended the affair.

In recent years revolts have been less colourful. Sometimes they are concerned with the appointment or dismissal of a master. Thus a secondary modern school went on strike a few years ago as a protest against their sports master, and a little later, in contrast, the boys at a Grammar School demonstrated against the dismissal of their music master by booing the Head at morning assembly, refusing to sing the hymn, and chalking defiant slogans on blackboards and walls.*

This is at least a pale shadow of the old-time rebellions; but, when we recall the bombs and gunpowder plots that Dr Keate and Dr Ingles had to face, it is hardly more than a shadow. It is the spirit of revolt reduced from a bang to a whimper. Whether that is a good thing or a bad depends on whether we regard the process of education as a concert or a conflict.

* *Daily Telegraph*, February 6, 1954.

CHAPTER FIVE

WHOM THE GODS HATE

'IT is when the gods hate a man with uncommon abhorrence,' said Seneca, 'that they drive him into the profession of a schoolmaster.'

English schoolmasters have often said much the same themselves. 'A fruitless, wearisome, and unthankful office,' said an Elizabethan teacher; 'I wax utterly weary of my place, and my life is a continual burden to me.' 'A poor needy animal,' was Goldsmith's description of an usher; and he had the best of claims to be a judge. 'Unwelcome drudgery,' cried Thomas Cooper, an enthusiastic starter, after eight years of his country school in the eighteen-thirties. 'Thirty years' imprisonment!' exclaimed Dr Bernard Henderson after being released from his London grammar school in the nineteen-thirties. And some power has gied these men the giftie to see themselves as others see them. 'Never in my life,' said Reginald Hine (solicitor to a branch of the N.U.T.) after a teachers' conference, 'never in my life had I beheld a more dejected, disillusioned, hang-dog set of men.'

Although a good many individual teachers have been highly honoured and praised—and a few well rewarded—teachers as a class have often been viewed with dislike and paid with contempt. It is noteworthy how poor a figure schoolmasters present in Shakespeare's portrait gallery. Holofernes is a pedantic ass, and even Sir Hugh Evans inspires tolerance rather than admiration. Elyot refers indignantly to 'ignorant schoolmasters' destroying the 'good and clean wits of children,' and suggests that many learned scholars avoid the profession of schoolmastering because it is 'so much had in contempt.'

Henry Peacham, who had been a schoolmaster himself and
knew conditions from the inside, roundly condemns the many
'egregious tyrants' whose stupidity and brutality did so much
damage to decent lads. Goldsmith's eighteenth-century village
master is quite a personage, it is true;* but Goldsmith was
looking on the departed village scene through a rose-tinted
mist of time. Elsewhere he speaks of schoolmasters as 'generally
despised.' The good-natured but feeble Partridge does not
suggest that Fielding had any great respect for the village
master; while Crabbe's Reuben Dixon implies a positive
though not unkindly contempt for the master of the common
day school and his 'vain attempts to keep the peace' till the
bell tolls and 'strife and troubles cease.'

One of the most impressive evidences of the general attitude
to schoolmasters in the eighteenth century is found in the
records of Gilbert Wakefield, an able controversial scholar
of slightly left-wing tendencies. 'It may be assumed,' he says
in his memoirs, 'as an indisputable proposition that no man
of taste and learning will ever keep a school but for *necessity*;
and therefore this task devolves upon poor curates in the church,
and poor ministers among the dissenters; men useful and
respectable in their proper functions, but, for the most part,
scantily furnished with polite literature. Hence it comes to
pass that a learned schoolmaster is rarely to be met with.'

Looking back over his own education he comes to the
deliberate conclusion that 'my acquisitions, in all these years,
from the abilities of my numerous teachers, were literally
nothing.'

Still, when all is said, a school is not really complete without
teachers; and this has been fully recognised by the founders
of our ancient schools. Their statutes and injunctions have
always contained provisions relating to the Master; and often
they were pretty stringent. He might be required, for example,
to be 'a man of wise sociable and loving disposition.' He
would usually be required to know Latin, and perhaps Greek

* He was based, it is said, on an old Quartermaster of Marlborough's wars.

too, 'if any such may be got.' Sometimes it was laid down
that he should be a B.A. or M.A., 'if it may be conveniently.'

Some of the specific requirements might seem at a glance
superfluous. Oundle, for instance, demanded a man who was
not 'a common gamester, haunter of taverns, neither to exceed
in apparel nor any other ways to be an infamy to the school.'
At Felsted the masters were not to be 'drunkards, whorehunters,
or lewd in living.' The founder of Chigwell School went
beyond these modest demands. 'I constitute and appoint that
the Latin schoolmaster be a graduate of one of the universities,
not under seven and twenty years of age, a Man skilful in the
Greek and Latin tongues, a good Poet, of a sound Religion,
neither Papist nor Puritan, of a grave Behaviour, of a sober
and honest Conversation, no Tipler nor Haunter of Ale
houses, no Puffer of Tobacco, and above all that he be apt
to teach and severe in his Government.'

Did the School ever obtain such a paragon? The records
do not say.

One might feel that the frequent insistence that the master
should be on the wagon was carrying things rather far. But it
was no casual injunction, nor an unnecessary one. At Sedburgh,
in the seventeenth century, the master was discovered to be
'a common frequenter of ale-houses . . . and hath been of late
negligent in his school, leaving the same for at least three
months together.'

Nor can this be put aside as an instance of typical seventeenth-
century debauchery, inspired by the dissipated Court of
Charles II, for the complaint was made during the rule of the
Puritans. Moreover, we have a similar charge in the early
reign of the virtuous Queen Victoria. In 1843 the Rev. John
Allen, one of the first school inspectors, reported of a school
in Radnorshire:

'I was told that the master was so far known to be addicted
to liquor that when one of the school trustees was expostulated
with on account of the master's being seen drunk in the streets,
it was answered that the quarterly payment of his salary had

D

just been made, and one must not be too severe in one's expectations at such a season.'

Even this sufferance of a teaching tippler leaves England a little in advance of at least one of her colonies. In Tasmania, in 1817, a magistrate's clerk was considered too much of a drunkard to retain his post: he was therefore granted a government salary so that he could set up as a schoolmaster.

Other strict requirements besides sobriety might be made by school founders. At Shrewsbury and St Bees, for example, a local man was at first insisted upon. Sometimes a clergyman was demanded; though, on the other hand, a few schools wanted a layman, free from the duties which a parson might have to perform. Occasionally the statutes were concerned about celibacy. At John Lyon's Harrow, for instance, if the master or usher married or 'be thought by the discretion of the greatest part of the Governors to be given to any notorious vice, they are instantly to be removed.' This was asking too much. Seventy years after Lyon's death the lesser evil was accepted, the rule against marrying being abolished, 'having by long experience proved to be very inconvenient.'

A foreshadowing of later Sickness Pensions was contained in the Shrewsbury Ordinance stating that any master 'infected with any lothesome, horrible, or contagious disease' was to be removed by the Bailiffs, and some charitable relief extended to him out of school revenues.

One matter on which every school formerly agreed was religion. Cleric or layman, the master had to be a man of sound religion, which meant that he had better not be too outspoken if he did not share the religious views of the government in power. From the twelfth century onwards the Church claimed, and received, the right to decide who should be allowed to teach. Even after Elizabeth's accession, it still remained the rule that any candidate for a teaching post had to be licensed by the Bishop of the diocese. Indirectly the regulation could have acted as a kind of examination for a Diploma in Pedagogy, if the Bishops had been interested

enough in education to make it so. It was a part of their task to
ensure that the candidate was 'meet as well for his learning
and dexterity in teaching as for sober and honest conversation.'
The Bishop could only make sure of these things by examining
the candidate. But the examination, where it took place at
all, was cursory, and an opportunity was lost for providing a
qualified teaching profession.

The Bishop's licence was not finally abolished—though
it had ceased to be effective—until 1869.

The bishop gave permission to teach, but he did not normally
appoint a master to a given school. In grammar schools (and
there were between three and four hundred of these in Elizabeth's reign) masters might be appointed by the founder or
his heirs, by royal authority, by some local or clerical body,
or by one of the university colleges.

One of the most notable schools of the Tudor period was
St Paul's, founded by Dean Colet in 1509. He deliberately
refrained from leaving his school in the care of the clergy of
his cathedral, having his own opinion about their reliability.
Instead he appointed the Company of Mercers to select the
Masters after his death, having found less corruption among
such citizens than among any other body of people. When a
suitable candidate had been discovered, 'a man whole in
body, honest and virtuous,' the Mercers were directed to
say to him: 'Sir, we have chosen you to be Master and Teacher
of this School, to teach the children of the same not only good
literature but also good manners . . . And every year at Candle-
mass, when the Mercers be assembled in the school-house, ye
shall submit you to our examination.'

Sometimes a master had to swear a solemn oath to carry
out his duties as a good teacher should, with a special clause
binding him to tread carefully on holy ground. 'I shall not
read to them any corrupt or reprobate books or works set
forth at any time contrary to the determination of the universal
Catholic Church, whereby they may be affected in their youth
in any kind of heresy or corrupt doctrine.' This was at Kirkby

Stephen in 1566, but the same kind of oath was sworn at various schools.

Sometimes there were entrance ceremonies, such as the one at Shrewsbury, where the newly-appointed master delivered a Latin oration, and was welcomed by one of the best scholars in Latin, promising obedience on behalf of the pupils. At this particular school the proceedings ended on an all-friends-together note, the Bailiffs drinking the schoolmaster's health and the schoolmaster pledging his predecessor and the scholars.

Unfortunately this genial spirit was far from universal. Sometimes there were scandals, squabbles, and riots connected with the appointment of a new master. These, strange as it may seem, were often connected with salaries—not because the master was disgusted at the low rate of payment but because he was so anxious to get his fingers on the pickings that he and his supporters would stop at nothing to secure the appointment.

Teachers have invariably, and often with justice, complained that they are badly paid; but in certain schools in times past the master has been in the money. Where the salary was linked with property, a steady rise in prices meant that the value of the property concerned, and with it the salary, was enormously inflated, to the good fortune of the master.

One of the most remarkable instances of this was at Skipton Grammar School, Yorkshire. In 1550 the master's post was worth about £14, which was quite a fair sum in its day. The Master at Christ's Hospital, an unusually large school, received only £15; the average salary was nearer £7. Two hundred years later inflation had brought the £14 to £150, which, even allowing for the considerably decreased value of money, was still a very handsome sum.

In 1751 the existing Master (who also, rather curiously, held a living in far away Cumberland) was dying. Before he could expire two eager candidates were grasping for the spoils.

The Master was chosen by the Vicar and twelve church-wardens. Wardenship seems to have been a profitable occupation, for bribes up to £60 were offered by one of the candidates, William West. Apart from a certain amount of ready money he seems to have had no other qualifications for the post. His rival, the Rev. Stephen Barrett, indignantly condemned this bribery and corruption, 'the worst of national vices,' and considered 'the giver of bribes almost equally as guilty as the receiver.' Writing to a friend he declared that he could not think of competing on such terms, adding that with the help of the chief Trustee of the school (Lord Thanet) it should not be necessary anyhow.

By the end of the week, having dined with Lord Thanet and discovered that the noble lord's influence was less commanding or less ready than he had supposed, Mr Barrett's hatred of bribery was a little diminished. It was his duty to become Master of Skipton Grammar School, he felt, lest a less worthy person be appointed; and he was now willing to out-bribe his opponent if necessary, provided that the corruption was carried out in perfect secrecy. Alas, it was not; and fearing that the wardens (some of whom had cheerfully sold their votes to both sides) were becoming indiscreet about his promises to pay, Barrett withdrew from the field.

In the meantime two new candidates had appeared, one of whom, the Rev. Thomas Carr, with a modified offer of £40 and a cask of brandy, had gained the support of half the wardens against his rival, a local curate. Voting being even, a deadlock ensued; and according to the Founder's deeds the right of appointment now fell legally to the Fellows of Lincoln College, Oxford. They promptly appointed one of themselves, the Rev. Samuel Plomer. Carr had already dashed off to York to get the necessary Archbishop's licence to teach. He failed; but being a young man of initiative and persistence he assumed possession of the school in spite of not having been appointed and not possessing a teacher's licence. The assistant master's support was secured by the offer of a rise in salary.

Carr had been teaching for about three weeks when Plomer arrived, claiming, with some justice, to be the official master;

whereupon the school was closed and put into a state of siege, all doors being locked and bolted. Plomer and his local supporters did their best to surprise or overthrow the garrison. 'Several clandestine methods as well as open violence were used to get possession of the schoolhouse,' Carr complained to a friend; but the self-appointed and unlicensed teacher contrived to hold his position till the summer of 1752.

At length a truce was made. Plomer was allowed to assume the reins of office, apparently on the understanding that Carr should follow him when he retired. The pupils, who had enjoyed a year's holiday in the meantime, returned to school to pick up the threads of their rather haphazard education. Carr, in fact, had to wait twenty-eight years for his Mastership, but he achieved it in the end, and, moreover, held it for twelve years after Plomer's death. Throughout the whole period, including the siege of the grammar school, he was a curate of Bolton Abbey.

By the time of his death in 1792 the value of the Mastership had risen to £320 a year, more than double the 1751 value, and over twenty times its value in the sixteenth century. The scramble for this lucrative post became even more eager than it had been before, and the result was even more unfortunate for the education of Skipton's children. The grammar school remained closed for four years while the contestants for the mastership fought out their claims.

The most vigorous of the claimants was the Rev. Richard Withnell, curate at the parish church. He was eagerly supported by his vicar, partly, it may be, out of kindness of heart, partly because he was eager to get the curate off his hands and save his salary. In spite of secret meetings, stormy threats, and the reckless bribing of some of the wardens (up to £100 was offered for each vote), Withnell only just managed to carry the day. The keys of the school, unfortunately, were in the care of the father of one of the rival candidates, but the redoubtable vicar secured a locksmith and forced the doors.

All Withnell had to do now was to hurry off to York to

secure the Archbishop's licence to teach. This journey he duly made; but he had to return without the licence. The Archbishop, already informed of the scandals of the election, and perhaps genuinely uncertain of the successful candidate's suitability (he was not a university man), claimed the right to investigate Withnell's morals, religion, and learning. Withnell refused to put his learning to the test. A parish meeting was held again at Skipton at which Withnell was once more elected Master, after a certain troublesome warden had been made too drunk to know what he was doing. The Fellows of Lincoln College again wanted to appoint their own man, but after a lengthy legal dispute, more profitable to the law than to the school, Withnell was adjudged to have been legally appointed.

It was three years since the Mastership had fallen vacant, and the pupils had been waiting in vain for instruction. But even now the case was far from over. The Archbishop still refused to waive his right to examine Withnell's suitability for the post. A new legal contest began, this time Withnell versus the Archbishop of York. It was an important case, for if the Archbishop was not entitled to examine a candidate then his licence was a mere formality; and if, on the other hand, he *had* the right to refuse a licence, then, in effect, he could choose the Masters for all the schools in his diocese.

The judges decided in the Archbishop's favour in 1795, the Lord Chief Justice delivering a pronouncement which has since become notable in the history of education:

'Whoever will examine the state of the grammar schools in different parts of this kingdom will see to what a lamentable condition most of them are reduced, and would wish that those who have any superintendence or control over them had been as circumspect as the Archbishop of York on the present occasion. If other persons had equally done their duty we should not find, as is now the case, empty walls without scholars, and everything neglected but the receipt of salaries and emoluments.'

For four years the hungry sheep of Skipton had looked up at the closed doors of the grammar school, waiting in vain to be fed. Now the school reopened, with Lincoln College's new candidate as Master, and Withnell in retreat. But peace did not descend upon the school, and for many years to come there were disagreements and legal proceedings on the financial arrangements. The revenues from school lands, exploited by the Master, amounted to nearly £1,000.

Nominal evidence about public school salaries in the eighteenth and nineteenth centuries is apt to be very misleading. For example, at Eton, in 1730, the headmaster's official salary was £62, which even for those days seems an unimpressive figure for one of the leading public schools. But there was also an unofficial entrance fee for every boy in the school, and a yearly gratuity of four guineas from each upper school pupil, noblemen paying double. These fees were not actually demanded, and some boys did not pay them. But the majority did, and parents who were anxious for their son to make a good start in the school might do their best to smooth his path by plentifully greasing the headmaster's palm. It was also the custom for every boy who was leaving the school to show his appreciation of past favours by leaving a tip. In 1763 the headmaster received £411 from this source alone.

It becomes obvious that the headmaster in these cases had a very personal interest in keeping up the numbers in his school. The present 'points' system has enabled education to progress backwards to a rather similar position.

Assistant masters, too, were not confined to an official salary, if there was one. By all accounts, an Eton master might well be making a packet one way or another. For instance, a Mr Roberts in the eighteenth century undertook the charge of two or three boys of good family at the extravagant rate of £100 a year each. (Assistants were not then allowed to keep boarding-houses.) As his receipts from other pupils averaged £400 a year and he received £50 a year from the headmaster, his income as an Eton master was in the region of £700 a year, in addition to which he held a living in Northants. We have Goldsmith's evidence that a parson in that century could be passing rich on forty pounds a year, so it seems evident that Mr Roberts with over £700 a year might regard himself as quite a business magnate. Similarly, in 1818, an usher at Westminster, encouraging a friend to take over the job, gives the salary as being from £500-£800, including residence in a dame's boarding-house. As for the Rev. W. Richards, headmaster of Blundell's, he may fairly be regarded as the Rothschild of the teaching profession if there is any truth in the report that during his reign of twenty-six years he amassed £60,000!

But we must not ignore the other side of the medal. These were exceptional instances. Moreover, there were then—as there still are—persons who, when economies were needed, eagerly directed their gaze to the staff salary list. Schools founded for religious purposes were notably niggardly. 'Ours is not a cheap scheme for a national education,' wrote Nathaniel Woodard, referring to what is now the Anglican school, Lancing College, 'although *the cost of the teaching is cheap.*' (The italics are mine.) Equally characteristic is the attitude revealed by the Congregationalists in 1852, when their school at Lewisham (now Caterham School) found itself, by no means for the first time, in rough water. A specially appointed sub-committee put its finger at once on one obvious way of cutting down expenses. The master's salary was reduced by half, his meagre £200 a year becoming a far more meagre £100. The master, a man who had served the school for thirty years, and had several dependent children, was compelled to emigrate to Australia to begin a new life at the age of 65.

It was the same spirit that had led Roger Ascham to exclaim three hundred years earlier:

'They gladly give two hundred crowns a year to their ostler and are loth to give two hundred shillings to their schoolmaster.'

Teachers may be said to fall into six types: the intimidating, the inanimate, the industrious, the incredible, the incompetent, and the incomparable.

Let us not save our good wine till last but put it on the table at once. In spite of Wakefield's 'indisputable proposition' (and it is certainly well supported) that people are driven into teaching by desperation rather than by desire, it remains true that even from early times relations between teacher and taught have sometimes been warm to the point of affection. Alcuin, the adviser of Charlemagne, pays tribute to the learning and kindliness of his master at the cathedral school of York in A.D. 740. Thomas Tusser, though ruthlessly thrashed by Udall at Eton in the 1530's, had previously been happy under John Redford at St Paul's choir-school. In Shakespeare's time, Master Downhale of Christ's School, Gloucester, showed great familiarity and gentleness to at least one of his pupils, who reciprocated with reverence and love; though it is fair to add that this teacher soon found schoolmastering an unsatisfying job and forsook it to become secretary to the Lord Chancellor. Francis Goode, usher at Eton from 1717 to 1734, much beloved by his pupils, had 'an easy and pleasant way of instilling his instructions into the boys, who seemed rather to be entertaining themselves than at school while he was explaining Ovid and Terence to them.' Robert Thicknesse, Master of St Paul's in mid-eighteenth century, 'considered boys as rational beings, to be governed by reason, not by the rod.' Leigh Hunt, who dreaded his usual master, the notorious James Boyer, was transported with delight when his place was temporarily taken by the Rev. Mr Steevens, short, fat, and genial. 'You loved him as you looked at him.'

The Rev. W. Tuckwell, who was a boy at Winchester in 1840, recorded a pleasing episode concerning Charles Wordsworth (the poet's nephew), Second Master and afterwards headmaster of the College. 'He once found me, a boy of fourteen, sitting alone in the schoolroom, reading a book and eating a cake. He sat down by me, talked about the book, and shared laughingly a few morsels of my confection. Next day from La Croix's [the tuck shop] came a pile of sponge cake and cream.' It is true that the gift was accompanied by a Greek epigram, but Wordsworth (and some of his scholars) had learned almost to think in Latin and Greek.

Then there was the Rev. John Smith of Harrow (1854–82), 'the most saintly schoolmaster in recorded history,' whose very name evoked a burst of spontaneous cheering at an Old Boys' gathering. 'To his generous sympathy,' wrote J. A. Symonds, 'I ascribe the only pure good of my Harrow training.' He was a parson who really lived his religion; but, alas, he died in a mental home. There was Dean Farrar, also of Harrow, 'whose mental sympathies,' wrote one of his pupils, 'were simply boundless if a boy chose to work.' There was Caldwell Cook of Perse School, Cambridge, in whose originating hands the famous Play Way was not a method of avoiding work but a way of living.

Nor must we neglect to look for gold among the Cockneys. George Lansbury was sent to a little private school in White-chapel some eighty years ago, run by a Nonconformist minister with a freely-used strap. 'I remember nothing of any worth which I learnt at this school, except what was taught us by a nice little kind old man who made the most wicked and unruly of us love him. He came every Friday to give us history lessons. This teacher made the historic scenes, such as Alfred's struggles with the Danes, the Conqueror's landing at Hastings . . . actually live before our eyes. I have never met his like since.'

Teachers of this sort have been discoverable in every age. Friendliness was not a virtue that came in with the Butler Act of 1944. The old schoolmaster was not always an old tyrant.

This needs to be said. Having said it, we must squarely face the fact that these incomparable teachers are not those whose names and portraits spring most readily to mind when we hear the words pedagogue, master, or beak.

Foremost, I suppose, come the intimidators, brandishing their fists and their rods. More will be said of them in a chapter devoted to their punishment habits, but they must be touched upon here.

One of the worst, surely, was Robert Crayford, usher at Perse School in the middle of the seventeenth century. In 1652 he took complete charge of the school until the appointed headmaster, George Griffiths, could take over. Crayford was annoyed at not being offered the headship; and he first relieved his feelings by an assault on the new headmaster, whom he openly called a stinking knave, and to whom, in front of the pupils, he threatened to give a kick in the pants. ('I will take you a kick on the britch!')

To what extent, if at all, the boys objected to this we have no record; but they certainly objected to his treatment of themselves. A boy named Peters was handled worse than an animal in a slaughter-house. He was 'wrung by both his eares in such violent manner that one of his eares was cruelly torne both skin and grissle, and almost went from his head.' He fled home with the blood running down from his head to his feet. Another time the master thrashed a boy so severely 'that he could scarce endure to lay himself down in his bed at night.' The father complained without effect, and at last was compelled to take his son from the free school and send him to a private school. A third pupil, the son of a surgeon, was almost battered into lunacy. 'And the said Robert Crayford did smite one Edward Webb in a most violent manner upon his jawes, and beat hym downe with his head against a wooden forme. Webb rising up again, Crayford smote him a second time in like manner.' For a time the boy was said to be in danger of death, and perhaps recovered only through his father's skill. But his speech and memory remained so affected that his career as a scholar came to an end.

One wonders why the parents did not combine to give this ferocious savage some of his own treatment. Perhaps the fact that they did not is itself an indication of the kind of behaviour that was regarded as natural to a pedagogue. He was, indeed, dismissed from his post in 1653, but he refused to leave his house, and, incredibly, he found local persons ready to support him. Not until 1656 was he made to go, and then only after protracted and expensive legal action and by a compromise agreement which allowed him to stay on in the usher's house for a year after the appointment of his successor.

No doubt the more violent excesses of schoolmasters were checked by the law. Indeed, a legal treatise of the late eighteenth century (Burns's *Justice of the Peace*) warns masters not to go too far; though the implications of the warning are themselves grim enough. 'Where a schoolmaster, in correcting his scholar, happens to occasion his death, if in such correction he is so barbarous as to exceed all bounds of moderation, he is at least guilty of manslaughter; and if he make use of an instrument improper for correction, as an iron bar or sword, or if he kick him to the ground, and then stamp on his belly, and kill him, he is guilty of murder.' It is a relief, and indeed a surprise, to find that there were at least some limits to the master's right to correction.

Still, there remained plenty of scope. William Birch, master of the Lower Third at Rugby in the last decade of the eighteenth century, in addition to having a name that was in itself a threat, had also, it is said, 'a fist like a sledge-hammer, which he made pretty free use of.' William Page of Westminster, 'savage and ill-tempered,' had been actually seen to lift a boy off the ground by his ears. Boyer of Christ's Hospital, in the front rank of the bullies, was another ear-attacker. 'You may easily imagine,' writes one of his pupils, 'what an impression it produced on me when, within a day or two of my first taking my seat in the school, I saw him take a little boy by the ears and pinch him till the poor fellow roared and shrieked with agony. There were many who could show on their ears the marks of the tyrant's thumb-nails.'* One feels that a scrum-

* W. P. Scargill.

cap should have formed an essential part of every schoolboy's equipment.

It was Boyer who had the distinction of bringing up that great trio of Old Blues, Coleridge, Lamb, and Leigh Hunt. The former, with his head in the clouds, persuaded himself that his old master was severe but just. Lamb, writing as a conventional wearer of the Old School Cravat, referred euphemistically to Boyer as having 'a temper a little too hasty to leave the more nervous of us quite at our ease to do justice to his merits.' But going in to bat a second time he abandoned these fanciful understatements and spoke out more like an honest man: 'I have known Boyer double his knotty fist at a poor trembling child with a "Sirrah, do you presume to set your wits at me?"' Leigh Hunt had no equivocations at all. He frankly bears out Scargill's report of brutality: 'He had a trick of pinching you under the chin, and by the lobes of the ears until he would make the blood come. He has many times lifted a boy off the ground in this way . . . I have seen him beat a sickly-looking, melancholy boy (C——n) about the head and ears, till the poor fellow, hot, dry-eyed, and confused, seemed lost in bewilderment. C——n, not long after he took orders, died, out of his senses.'

Boyer's successor, Edward Rice, seems to have inherited some of his precursor's talents.

'To see that man of the fist, rod, and cane spending his force on a little boy, leaving the autograph of his four fingers, in red and white, on the infant's cheek, sending him reeling half-way up the room, was a sight worthy of the demons.'*

It is only fair to add that D'Arcy Thompson, author of that semi-classic, *Day-dreams of a Schoolmaster*, while admitting that the younger boys feared Rice, maintained that 'his heart was of the kindest and softest'; but Thompson was a sixth-form favourite. To the ordinary boy a hard hand is not redeemed by a soft heart.

It is not improbable that Rice's mind was affected by his

* T. G. Hake.

work. Within a week of his retirement he hanged himself from his bed-post.

While Hake was trembling under Rice's fist in Newgate Street, William Ballantine (afterwards a distinguished lawyer) was enduring education at the neighbouring school of St Paul's, which at this time possessed three undermasters named Bean, Edwards, and Durham. 'They possessed one common attribute: they were all tyrants—cruel, cold-blooded, unsympathetic tyrants. Armed with a cane and surrounded by a halo of terror, they sat at their respective desks.' A favourite trick of all three was to strike the boys on the tips of their frozen fingers when they entered school, shivering and gloveless, on a cold winter's day. Bean was perhaps the worst of the three, 'a short, podgy, pompous man of insignificant features . . . I can see him now, with flushed, angry face, lashing some little culprit over the back and shoulders until his own arm gave way under the exertion. Among the amusements of this gentleman, one was to throw a book at the head of any boy who indulged in a yawn, and if he succeeded in his aim and produced a reasonable contusion, he was in a good humour for the rest of the day.'

The passing years have diminished the numbers of this type, and the nation's laws have curbed his hand. But he has never died out altogether, and perhaps never will.

He may be found in any type of school. Mr Squeers and Mr Creakle, made vivid by Dickens's imagination but based on reality, are the unforgettable fictional representatives of the private school; and here is a companion from real life—the music master at a certain college in Canterbury in the 1890's. 'As his pupils with fear and trembling played their appointed pieces, he would beat time with a ruler, and whenever we failed to keep time the ruler would beat down on our wrists.' If the performer struck a wrong note he would receive a violent cuff over the head from the master's other hand, often so forceful as to knock him clean off the piano-stool. 'Once,' says Reginald Hine, 'in performing Mendelssohn's *Songs*

Without Words I hit the ground six times.' But Hine was a future lawyer; and already there was a different attitude towards pedagogic bullies. He organised a petition among the boys whose parents paid extra for music, and slipped it through the headmaster's letter-box. The music master soon afterwards left the school.

Just occasionally the bully provokes retaliation. An unpopular Maths master at the same school, with a pointed head and a square jaw, known to his victims as 'the isosceles triangle,' used constant sarcasm as his chief weapon. One day a hot-headed Jamaican boy, taunted beyond bearing, sprang suddenly from his desk and began butting the master in the stomach. This was the one form of attack to which the master, who was 6 ft. 2 in. tall, was vulnerable. The combatants staggered about the room, the one trying to protect his middle, the other bleeding freely from the nose. The master's desk went over; ink spurted everywhere. The boy's collar and tie were ripped; the master's gown was torn in strips, and his glasses were clawed to the ground and trampled under foot. One of his eyes followed his assailant's movements, but the other gazed straight ahead, unblinking. Then, to the shocked amazement of the class, it fell out and rolled across the floor.

At this moment the headmaster entered. The silence was overpowering. After surveying the scene without a word, he quietly picked up the glass eye, handed it to the master, and went out again.

So much for the intimidators. In the very nature of things there is little to be said of the inanimate. They survive their working hours with as little bother to themselves as they can, and go their way. We will link them with the industrious, for most teachers are a blend of the two, the latter element predominating.

The average teacher who gets on with his job but has no outstanding qualities is not always appreciated at his true worth, and is too soon forgotten by the average pupil. Every-one, on the other hand, remembers the incredibles—the eccentrics in dress, manner, and speech. They are not easily caught in a writer's net, but most schools in the past had at least one or two specimens fluttering round the staff common room. A few still survive, even in efficient State schools.

Such, no doubt, was 'Judy' Durnford, Lower Master at Eton in the 1860's and 1870's, 'a sort of weatherbeaten Ancient Mariner in academic garb,' a tall man with trousers that were always too short and white socks that were consequently too prominent, especially in conjunction with black shoes. The lower boys became used to his strange appearance and his queer nasal voice, especially as it was one of his duties to flog them, which he did efficiently enough. But his oddity needed familiarity to make it easily palatable. When on one occasion he unexpectedly took prayers with the Collegers, in the Head's absence, he had barely begun when the room was swept with a tornado of laughter. His peculiar voice was swallowed up by the merriment it produced. 'So disgraceful was the behaviour,' said one of the offenders, 'that, when prayers were concluded, the boys themselves rose sobered and ashamed.' Unfortunately, the master then gave a series of solemn head-shakes and exclaimed in a pained nasal tone, 'It's fearful to contemplate—fearful to contemplate,'—and laughter broke out afresh.

Peculiar in a different way was an earlier Eton master, B. H. Drury, such an enthusiastic lover of theatre and prize-ring that he used to slip off to London whenever he could. Drury was said to need as much supervision as any of the pupils. The headmaster one day went to his bedroom, having received a message that he was too unwell to attend school. He found Drury in bed, certainly, but fully dressed for a dash to London as soon as the coast was clear. He was as fond of fighting as of watching it; and on one occasion, after a theatre visit with a colleague and a couple of pupils, he embroiled his companions in a fracas with a watchman. All four had to be bailed out of Bow Street, by the Lord Chancellor, whose son was one of the party. 'Drury drinks for ever' runs a line of an old lampoon, and it was probably not far from the truth. Another Eton master, William Heath, was an opium addict. A fourth, 'able but singular,' indulged in what must surely be the queerest way ever recorded of dealing with the offer of a job. Uncertain whether to accept or not, instead of leaving it to the toss of a coin, he wrote two letters, one accepting the appointment, the other refusing it. He then shuffled them, and put one letter in the post and the other in the fire, without any idea which was which.

Harrow also had its oddities, among whom must be included a different Drury (Henry), whose passion was not for fighting but for fires. He would go any distance to see one. When the Houses of Parliament were burnt down in 1834 he left his class and hurried off to the churchyard, where he sat for three hours watching the blaze. He was also, it seems, fond of his bed—so fond that it became customary to send a fag to his house each morning to find out if he was getting up. If not the boys would turn over in their own beds and have another sleep.

Another odd Harrow master was the Rev. Mr Middlemist, who was so suspicious of everybody that he would not even let another person post a letter for him. He took violent dislikes to pupils for the most trivial reasons, had a genius for picking out the most innocent boy in the class as the target for his chief attacks, and made the boys in his House football team eat the stodgiest possible pudding before a match—either from a dislike of football or from a dislike of boys.

A third Harrow man combined eccentricity with the most sublime autocracy. Two young members of his House were discovered one winter's evening, after dusk, sitting by the road-side. The master who saw them asked what they were doing. 'We were late for lock-up,' they told him, 'and Mr B—— won't let us in.' The master rang the door-bell, prepared to expose this most improbable tale. Mr B—— himself answered the door, and impatiently interrupted his colleague's attempt to investigate.

'The rules of the school,' he snapped, 'are that boys must be in by lock-up. These boys were not. I therefore decline to accept them now.' And he slammed the door.

As it seemed neither ethical nor expedient to leave two boys sitting in the road all night the master took them to the headmaster, H. M. Butler.

'There must be some mistake,' said Dr Butler. 'Let them sit in my hall while I send a note to Mr B——'

But there was no mistake. Mr B—— was determined to be master in his own House; and his reply to the headmaster echoed his reply to his colleague. He did in the end haul down his flag, but it took several increasingly warm notes from Dr Butler before this was achieved.

The master who walks by himself, like Mr B—— of Harrow, is troublesome enough; but he is less of a pain in the neck to his colleagues than the man who is always deliberately out of step. Such was Mr K——, who (so R. C. Robertson-Glasgow tells us) took a violent dislike to all the other members of the staff at his Hindhead prep school some thirty years ago. One way in which he showed his feelings was to give ridiculously low marks when examining another master's pupils. Thus the brightest boy in the class was found to have gained only twelve marks out of a hundred. This anti-social scheme was countered by multiplying all Mr K——'s marks by seven; whereupon he resigned in a huff. He probably suffered from some kind of religious mania, and used to tell his pupils that if they got their sums wrong they would never go to the heavenly mansions, a moral which was spoilt by his pointing upwards— to the dormitories.

The Rev. E. E. Bryant, of Charterhouse, also used to castigate his pupils for idleness; but he would then suddenly exclaim aloud: 'But who am I to apportion blame and to find fault? Bryant, you have been a sinner yourself!' At these outbursts, one of his former pupils tells us, no one in the class thought of laughing or being embarrassed. It was accepted as perfectly natural to 'Eb.' He used periodically to retire behind the blackboard during lessons: the class were convinced that he was having a private fight with the devil. Another master at this school used to stand behind the goal of the opposing side in House matches, making discouraging remarks to the goalkeeper. At cricket he would stand behind the bowler's arm, first at one end, then at the other, when two of the opposing batsmen appeared to be set. This master had a glass eye which was once mislaid, and which once disturbed a lesson by falling out on the classroom floor, like the eye of the 'isosceles triangle' but without the provocation.

Masters with glass eyes and short-sighted masters almost inevitably bring themselves into the ranks of the eccentrics. Those of the second sort are legion; and one representative must suffice. He was at Hurst College in the middle of last century.

'At frequent intervals [says the record] the two staffs of Shoreham and Hurst (Hurstpierpoint) used to meet together for a joint conference. The Rev. Frederick Mertens had no sense of taste or smell, and Pennell, one of the Hurst masters, was almost blind. Mertens was bending down low over his food to scrutinise it (his method of testing food owing to his defective sense of taste), and Pennell, dimly seeing Mertens' clerical collar almost on the table, mistook it for the rim of his tea-cup and proceeded to pour milk down Mertens' neck.'

Perhaps another Lancing master should be included among the eccentrics—A. C. Wilson, who one day found a boy pulling another boy's nose. 'He put the offending boy's nose under the lid of a desk and sat on it.'

It not infrequently happens that the senior master—perhaps through long service, perhaps through disappointment at failing to secure a headship—develops certain singularities. Thus Howard Candler, senior master of Uppingham in the 'eighties, a very small man who wore a semi-clerical dress, never walked from place to place but advanced with a most peculiar trot: one of his colleagues described him as the only man he knew who could walk with one leg and run with the other. Instead of carrying his books in the normal way with his arm at waist level, he held them with his left arm bent up to the level of his shoulder. Nor was he free from mental incoherence. 'To the end,' a younger colleague and ex-pupil recorded, 'he used to confuse me with my uncle, who was five-and-thirty years my senior.'

Billy Oxenham, nearly forty years on the staff at Harrow (he retired in 1863), was another senior master whose ways induced mirth rather than respect. He was no disciplinarian, we are told, and was unsuccessful as a teacher. Bullying was rife in his House. His particular eccentricity was a habit of uttering a series of 'Damns' on the slightest provocation. The boys in his own House used to turn this peculiarity to advantage by scattering tacks on the stairs when they wished to engage in some unlawful dormitory activity. Then Oxenham, creeping upstairs in his stockinged feet, would be heard crying 'Damn! Damn! Damn!' with such involuntary warmth as to give them adequate warning. Relations between him and his third headmaster, C. J. Vaughan, were not cordial. 'Damn the fool! Damn the fool!' he would cry when the headmaster's activities were mentioned. Vaughan, for his part, would not let his Second Master (and deputy) have access to new birches for flogging, but, contrary to custom, made him use second-hand ones.

And finally, by not a very formidable jump, to the corner of the staff room inhabited by the hopelessly incompetent, despised by their colleagues and baited by their pupils.

Such as, for example, Mr Hayes, usher of the Fifth Form at Westminster in Southey's day, with whom the boys took impudent liberties, 'sticking his wig full of paper darts, and, indeed, doing or leaving undone whatever they pleased.' Perhaps we should include his predecessor earlier in the century, Vincent Bourne, good-natured, indolent, slovenly, and weak—so slovenly that William Cowper remembered seeing a boy set fire to his greasy wig, and so weak that the same boy boxed the master's ears to put out the flames. (But, let it not be forgotten, the poet loved the memory of Vinny Bourne, and highly esteemed his Latin verses.) Then there was Mr Jeudwine, the second master of Shrewsbury School in the great Dr Butler's day, who used to find himself stuck to his chair with cobbler's wax.

When the stronghold of the Classics began to be penetrated, though feebly enough, by such minor innovations as French and Mathematics, it became the custom for pupils to mark the insignificance of these subjects by mocking the masters who took them. Teachers of the Classics, among whom head-masters were always included, gave tacit support to the ridicule even if they did not actually join in.

Thus at Westminster in the 1770's a boy deliberately dropped a dictionary from an upper window on the head of the French master. He was sent to the headmaster, Dr Smith, for punishment.

'Oh, but sir,' the boy excused himself, 'it was only a Frenchman.'

'A Frenchman, eh?' said the Doctor good-humouredly. 'Very well, then, go and sit down.'

An insular contempt for foreigners no doubt partly inspired this attitude, which was naturally strengthened during and after the Napoleonic Wars.

'It was thought a good joke at that time [Winchester College in the 1840's] to say "Waterloo" to a Frenchman. The master was M. Arnati, a good fellow probably in private life but with a capacity for furious anger . . . The spell tried on M. Arnati never failed.' The master used to rush at his worst tormentor with a cane, striking blindly, while the boy dodged him under desks and forms, and the whole class encouraged the combatants. It was typical, if not deliberate, that when the school had to endure two separate hours of supervised preparation on holidays (11 till 12, and 4 till 5), the grim task of superintendence was pushed on to the unfortunate French master, who (it is not surprising to learn) 'had rather a warm time of it.'

Jacob Marillier, who endured an incredibly long service at Harrow (1819–62), combined the disadvantages of being a Frenchman and teaching Maths in what was to him a foreign tongue. He lived the life of a dog, being 'received with hallooing and hooting whenever he appeared.'

An Italian master at Eton in the 'seventies received quite different treatment. He was completely ignored, mainly because the boys who took Italian did so only in order to have extra time to cram for an examination in some more important subject. The only attention they gave the Signor was to look up, when he was trying to gain their attention, and politely ask him not to speak so loudly as it was disturbing their work.

It is naturally hard for a foreigner to feel quite at home in the atmosphere of an English school, particularly the rarified atmosphere of a public school. Methods of punishment inevitably present difficulties. Thus M. Rouge, at Uppingham in the 'eighties, found much of his hour taken up in writing a succession of notes to the housemasters of various offenders; but instead of making sure that each one was completed and duly delivered he would pass from one note to another. The boys turned this habit into a sport, the purpose of which was to divert in more than one sense.

M. Rouge had the habit of reading the note aloud as it was written. As he drew near the close it became a point of honour for a new culprit to distract the master's attention by committing an obvious and infuriating offence; whereupon M. Rouge would tear up his first note, and begin a second one devoted to the new offender. Once more, as this letter reached completion a third boy rushed into insubordination. At the end of the lesson the unlucky last wrong-doer was left with a completed letter of complaint to be delivered. However, as a rule the letter was otherwise disposed of, and nothing came of it.

This kind of tradition is hard to break. It continued long after enmity between France and England had ceased. In my own schooldays, when the two countries were hand in hand together on the battlefield, the wretched Frenchman who took us was regularly butchered in the old-fashioned way. Similarly at Harrow, where M. Minssen (1890–1921) tried to make his classroom a little corner of France but was defeated by disciplinary troubles. He was free enough with punishments, but was fooled by the boys into believing that twenty minutes' Punishment Drill in the Yard was a more dreaded penalty than being sent to the headmaster. A first offender threatened with a visit to the Head, would deliberately make himself a further nuisance, whereupon the master would exclaim angrily, 'Very well, you shall go to Punishment Drill instead!'

To masters in this unfortunate fifth category (and they are by no means all foreigners) punishment presents as many problems as instruction. If the master gives no punishment, his lenience or timidity are readily taken advantage of. If he does punish he is apt to punish the wrong boy, or to give the wrong punishment, or to punish too freely, or (most fatal) to fail to see that the punishment is duly performed.

And lastly, there is the question of remitting punishments, which may perplex other teachers besides the incompetent. If a man is kindly by nature, and many schoolmasters are, he is apt to suffer from uneasiness of conscience if, in a rush of irritation or flurry, he has dished out punishments that on second thoughts he feels were not really deserved. A good-natured man, too, is apt to give way to pressure from the victim.

One might expect that a boy released from an imposition or a detention would feel deeply grateful to his benefactor; but schoolboys sometimes have their own spirit of unreason. A thought-provoking instance comes from J. P. Graham, a nineteenth-century master at Uppingham. He was passing the window of a classroom one evening, and saw and heard a boy inside passionately arguing and pleading with a master. A little later, as Graham was returning, the boy came out and joined a friend who was waiting for him in the courtyard.

'Well, what did he say?' Graham heard the friend ask eagerly.

'It's all right,' said the pleader contemptuously. 'The silly fool let me off!'

CHAPTER SIX

UNEASY LIES THE HEAD

STRANGE as it may seem, the headmaster is quite a late entrant to the English school. From the earliest times to the days of Arnold the great man of the school was almost always known as 'the Master,' or 'the Schoolmaster,' his assistants, if any, being ushers or under-masters. (At Wellington College, even today, he is still 'the Master.')

Even after 'headmasters' had begun to appear, the word was a long time coming into popular use. Though Stanley's *Life of Arnold* refers often enough to the headmastership of Rugby, you will search in vain for any headmaster in *Tom Brown's Schooldays*. Arnold is always 'the Doctor.'

This is not merely a matter of terminology. The present-day conception of the headmaster as a man directing the affairs of the school from his study, and occasionally taking a Sixth Form lesson, is entirely modern. The Master was a teacher first and foremost, and even when he had one or more assistants he himself remained the sole teacher of the older boys, and this was his main job.

In most schools where a Second Master was officially appointed there was a clear division of responsibility. The Master's work was to look after the top of the school, and his colleague took charge of the rest, and was a king in his own right. It was no part of the Master's task to supervise the work of the whole school.

The Reverend James Boyer, Upper Master of Christ's Hospital in Charles Lamb's day, and as dominating a tyrant as any school ever possessed, shared a schoolroom in the usual eighteenth-century way, with the Lower Master, the Reverend

Matthew Field. Field's classes did just as they pleased. 'There was now and then the formality of saying a lesson,' but it mattered little to the master whether the pupil had learnt it.

Though he had charge of the whole classical education of a hundred children for the first four or five years of their Bluecoat School careers, Field spent much of his time in his own room, and often stayed away from the school for days, leaving his pupils to their own devices. In due course many of these neglected scholars passed on to Boyer, who had thus to build on foundations which could at best be called shaky. Boyer was by nature neither good-natured nor tolerant. Yet, Lamb tells us, 'he always affected, perhaps felt, a delicacy in interfering in a province not strictly his own,' and Field's Lower School pupils continued to live a life as careless as birds.

Even where the Master found himself unable to tolerate his junior colleague's inefficiency, he could rarely take direct action. There was no collecting up the neglected class's exercise books at the week-end and giving the teacher a dressing-down on Monday morning. Dr Burton, Master of Winchester College for over forty years, complained, in his fifteenth year of office (1739), that his usher, the Rev. Christopher Eyre, was not doing his job. 'The scholars at the Usher's end of the School do not make due progress in their learning,' he protested. But all he could do was to introduce an extra assistant to make good the deficiency by acting as a ramp to raise the ill-taught scholars to the level he required before taking them over.

Far from being ashamed at this oblique but pungent rebuke, the usher was greatly indignant at what he regarded as unwarrantable interference with his own concerns. When he discovered that two of his pupils had been taken from his class and put with the new assistant he flew after them and ordered them back. It is true that Mr Eyre ultimately resigned, but this was not the dismissal of a rebellious junior by his headmaster; it was a quarrel between two virtually independent masters.

The same independence lasted well into the nineteenth century. The famous Samuel Butler of Shrewsbury, whose name comes almost inevitably into any list of great headmasters, was in fact not a headmaster at all in the modern sense of the term. He was essentially a teacher. The fame he brought to the school was due entirely to the fact that he was one of the greatest classical scholars of his day and had a genius for imparting scholarship to his pupils. So little was he a head-master—the captain of a scholastic ship—that he remained at loggerheads with his Second Master, Mr Jeudwine, for thirty-seven years, and could do nothing to remove him. Butler wished to control the teaching methods and disciplinary arrangements throughout the school: Mr Jeudwine, an inferior scholar and a hopeless disciplinarian, refused to concede that the master of the upper school had any right to interfere with the lower school, and went his own way.

Let us consider a few of the more famous Masters who paved the way for future 'headmasters.'

One of the first to make a reputation was Nicholas Udall, in charge of Eton from 1534 to 1541. Students of literature know him as the author of the first English comedy. There was, however, nothing comic about his schoolmastering. He seems to have been a more literate Mr Squeers. A violent flogger of the traditional breed, he once pounced upon a new boy (if the victim is to be credited) and gave him fifty strokes for a trifling misdemeanour. Yet his attitude to his work left much to be desired, if his own words are to be credited, and his character would hardly, one would have thought, have per-suaded the most broad-minded prelate to bestow on him a teacher's licence. After seven years as Master of Eton he was sent to the Marshalsea Prison for scandalous immorality.

The powerful friends who had no doubt got him into Eton now got him out of prison. But their efforts to have him reinstated in his former post were unavailing, despite an effusive letter that he addressed to his former employers.

'Accept,' he pleaded, 'this mine honest change from vice to virtue, from prodigality to frugal living, from negligence of teaching to assiduity, from play to study, from lightness to gravity.'

Although this convenient repentance did not satisfy Eton it was good enough for Westminster, which accepted him, in Bloody Mary's reign, as a fit and proper person to take charge of its scholars. But the pain of changing from vice to virtue, or perhaps from negligence to assiduity, was too much for him. He died within a year.

One of Udall's pupils at Eton was Richard Mulcaster, who followed his master into the teaching profession and into the pages of the literary text-books. He became the first Master of Merchant Taylors School, where he stayed for twenty-five years, and then, as was the custom for several centuries, retired to the comfort of a country vicarage. Ten years later, at an age when today he would be compulsorily retired, he took charge of St Paul's School, and held on to the post for twelve years.

The fruit of his experience at Merchant Taylors was embodied in two notable educational books, the *Positions* and the *Elementarie*. In an age when the study of the classics was the whole of education, Mulcaster pleaded for the use of the English tongue: 'I love Rome, but London better; I honour the Latin, but I worship the English.' One of his pupils subsequently helped to justify this faith in the importance of English by writing 'The Fairie Queene.'

In spite of his love for English, Mulcaster's job was to teach Latin grammar as laid down in the Statutes, not to make experiments in the curriculum. He carried out this no doubt irksome labour with typical Elizabethan thoroughness and brutality, making Latin almost synonymous with lashes.

The same principles of education were still commonly employed in the following century. The most famous head-master of the period, Richard Busby, was also the most notable flogger. 'I see great talents in that sulky boy,' he said of Robert

South, afterwards a famous preacher, 'and my rod shall bring them out of him.' This was the essence of his method.

Busby, however, was something more than a brute teaching Latin with a birch in his hand. The fact that he taught—as has been claimed—the greatest architect, the greatest philosopher, and the greatest poet of the century* may have been due to luck. That he taught thirteen (some say sixteen) of the Bench of Bishops was no doubt because Westminster at that time was the favourite school of the ruling classes. But only a man of uncommonly commanding or persuasive character could have held on for fifty-seven years (a record for headmastership) to a school which, by its position, was so intensely close to the heart of seventeenth-century religion and politics—and this throughout the most troubled and turbulent period of English history.

Let us, by way of contrast, look at the career of Thomas Chaloner, who became Master of Shrewsbury School three years before Bushby took charge of Westminster. Though Chaloner made a success of his work and considerably increased the school's numbers, he was summarily thrown out of his post by the Puritans in 1645, and set up an independent school in the same county. Driven from this, he went to London and paid £60 to reinstate himself with the Commonwealth, after which he set up a new school in Shrewsbury, taking forty pupils with him from his previous school and raising the number to nearly a hundred in a few months. The influence of a Parliamentary friend procured him the Mastership of Market Drayton Grammar School (though he had to persuade the existing Master to leave a vacancy by offering him a bribe of £10). But in due course he was hounded out of this by a Puritan committee, and he moved off, accompanied by twelve faithful pupils, to a school in distant Wales. The dreaded plague broke into his success here. Once again he moved, and then again, and then again, plague or Puritans for ever at

* Wren, Locke, and Dryden.

his heels. At last, after an exile of nineteen years, he returned to Shrewsbury School in 1663, too exhausted by his wandering life to survive more than another two years.

Throughout this period, and for another thirty years after it, Dr Busby reigned serenely at Westminster, taking Civil War, Puritanism, Restoration, Plague, Romanism, and Revolution equally in his stride. No doubt powerful friends in Parliament or at Court helped to keep him where he was in times of difficulty; but it argues a powerful personality to command such friends.

Busby was certainly a personage. It is well-known that when Charles II visited the school, Busby kept his hat on despite the monarch's presence, and afterwards explained to the King that it was not consistent with the dignity of his position to doff his hat to any man in front of his pupils. That is the spirit of headmastership in the grand style, and Busby was the first English schoolmaster to show it.

Perhaps the only schoolmaster before him to be as independent towards outsiders as he was intimidating to his pupils was Alexander Gill, Senior, High Master of St Paul's. But there was a wildness in Gill's arrogance that brings it nearer to eccentricity than to Busby's stately self-sufficiency. He was the most reckless flogger of all time, who used his vicious birch not only on his boys but, with their assistance, on any grown-ups who happened to offend him. In so far as we may trust that entertaining but not always reliable guide, John Aubrey, Gill whipped a passer-by when a stone was thrown through one of the school windows; and the victim was unable to retaliate on any future occasion because the Doctor never went out except to church, and then only in the company of his regiment of pupils. Strange as it may seem, the assaulted man was unable to obtain any legal redress.

According to a doggerel verse which Aubrey records, Dr Gill publicly thrashed his grown-up son, a university graduate, for a badly written letter to himself. Another sufferer, it seems, was Dr Thomas Triplett, a former pupil who was rash enough to pay a visit to his crusty old schoolmaster. What the provocation was, if any, Aubrey does not say.

Dr Triplett, who became master of a private school in Surrey, was as violent as his own master. One of his pupils, encouraged by a companion named George Ent, went one day to the master's study and begged for some honey, a pot of which had just been presented by the boy's mother.

'You audacious rascal,' said the Doctor, and gave him a hearty cuff on the ear. 'How dare you be thus impudent!'

Then, discovering that Ent was the instigator, he took a flying leap and literally kicked this wretched boy down a flight of stone steps. He fell on his head and might well have broken his neck. The only result, however, was that Mr Ent removed his son.

Sound and fury remained a traditional characteristic of Mastership for a good many years to come. Richard Roberts, of St Paul's, though an elderly man in the later period of his forty-five-year reign, regained his youth, we are told, when there was chastisement to be administered. 'When plying the cane he was wonderfully active, as if inspired by a new life.' Dr George Heath, headmaster of Eton at the very end of the eighteenth century, was a determined flogger of the Udall stamp, and a man undaunted by numbers. A letter written in 1798 mentions his having given fifty-two boys a round dozen each; and there is a tradition that on one occasion he flogged no fewer than 70 boys in succession, giving them ten cuts each, after which he was laid up with aches and pains for more than a week. He was never at a loss for a reason to bring the rod into action. A boy was flogged for striking a companion who had pulled his hair, and again for putting his foot against another boy's.

To a headmaster eager to assert his authority, any excuse for punishment was sufficient. Dr Gabell of Winchester, a contemporary of Dr Heath, once whipped a boy who was wearing a black handkerchief round his neck as a cure for a sore throat, on the ground that he had gone to bed with his clothes on.

The same type of man could be found in the smaller schools as in the great ones. Mr Hunter, Samuel Johnson's master at Lichfield, 'would beat a boy equally for not knowing a thing as for neglecting to know it. He would ask a boy a question, and if he did not answer it, he would beat him, without considering whether he had an opportunity of knowing how to answer it.' About the same period William Hutton, as a child of five, attended a school in Derbyshire whose master, Mr Thomas Meat, 'often took occasion to beat my head against the wall, holding it by the hair.' Mr Jones, the proprietor and headmaster of Dickens's private school at Camden Town, 'whose chief employment [says one of his pupils] was to scourge the boys,' was quite precisely and damningly portrayed as Mr Creakle, nursing the deadly mahogany ruler which struck fear into the heart of David Copperfield. The Nonconformist school in Whitechapel to which young George Lansbury went in the eighteen-sixties, was ruled over by a minister 'who opened his school with long prayers and kept us in order by frequent doses of punishment inflicted with a strap.'

But we must return to Eton to meet the most famous of the tyrants. Eight years after Dr Heath's retirement, early in the nineteenth century, Dr John Keate returned to the old tradition after an interlude by a more humane and courteous ruler. Something has already been written of Dr Keate, but more must be added, if only because attempts have been made by later Etonians to include him among the Arnolds and Thrings.

'Keate was in his way,' says the official Eton historian, 'a really great headmaster.' There is no justification for the claim. A great character, no doubt; but a headmaster whose attitude to his pupils is one of snarling mistrust cannot be ranked among the major figures in education. He flogged mercilessly. He had, said Kinglake, the power of quacking like an angry duck, and he normally spoke in this way in order to terrorise his pupils. His injustices, said Gladstone, dulled the

E

moral sense. He possessed, and constantly showed, a rooted distrust of his pupils' honour, and used to make random charges of lying. 'You're hardened in falsehood,' was one of his catch phrases; and the boys who are constantly accused of untruthfulness soon grow to deserve the charge.

Great headmasters are not fashioned out of such dirty clay. In spite of his lively activity and his undoubted courage, he was a bad influence on his school. Nor did the ill-humoured severity that he adopted succeed in taming his unruly mob. There is little evidence that the tone of the school improved under the shadow of his birch. It was probably better under Goodall, his predecessor, and certainly better under Hawtrey, his successor. The furious outbursts, the fierce floggings, were an incitement to rowdiness as much as a queller of rows. Booing was said to be a common accompaniment to Keate's harangues, until 'he got so inflamed in the face, and foamed and spurted from the mouth' to such an extent that he was expected to fall into a fit. Songs were sung during his lessons, without Keate being able to trace the culprits. Books, rotten eggs, and even stones were thrown at him. Feet were noisily shuffled and scraped in order to annoy him. The doors of his high desk were screwed up to keep him out, and on at least one occasion the desk was smashed to pieces.

Throughout the thirty-five years of his reign the birch rose and fell remorselessly and unremittingly. Flogging was, it has been said, the 'head and tail' of his system, and Sir Harry Bumper was no readier to find an excuse for the glass than Keate to find an excuse for the lash. A boy accused of an offence that he had not committed explained that he had been somewhere else at the time. 'Then I'll flog you for that!' cried Keate, and did so. Kept waiting on another occasion by a victim who failed to turn up for the execution, Keate was so furious that he seized a brother (some say namesake) of the culprit and flogged him instead.

Doubts have been cast on the authenticity of the familiar confirmation class story, but whether or not it is true in detail

Dr Keate

it shows the kind of thing that could easily happen under Keate's ferocious and mistrustful rule. A group of boys, it is said, one day turned up for a confirmation class with the Rev. Dr Keate, and the first boy handed the headmaster a list of their names on a piece of paper similar to the 'bill' on which offenders' names were always written. Keate promptly flogged the lot, giving them an extra severe thrashing for setting up a plea 'not only false but also irreverent.'

There is no question at all as to the authenticity of a mass flogging of the Fifth and Sixth Forms in the Library. An assistant master had complained that the Latin epigrams which these Forms were obliged to compose as an afternoon prep had all been written by two or three boys. Keate weighed in without hesitation, and flogged all seventy-two boys. 'It was a grand scene in the Library,' said an eye-witness. 'The floor was covered with the victims; the benches and tables with spectators; upward of a hundred present.' The Lower Boys were delighted to see their seniors whipped, and those victims who had often been flogged before were delighted to witness the punishment of those who had hitherto (miraculously) escaped the headmaster's birch. 'Jests and laughter accompanied the execution.'

It is clear that whatever Keate's qualities may have been, his approach to the business of education was as wrong as it could be. It is no doubt true that at heart he was a kindlier man

than his official snarl suggested, and it is certainly a fact that
at the end of his long headmastership the pupils subscribed
over £600 to buy him a leaving present, and cheered him
heartily. But schoolboys on such occasions, like B.B.C.
audiences at variety shows, will applaud anybody regardless
of merit; and a last-minute outburst of cheering does not
make Dr Keate a good headmaster, let alone a great one.

Nor can Keate's methods be excused on the grounds that
they were inevitable because of large classes or because of the
age in which he lived. That is nonsense. Such methods were
all too common before and even after the time of Dr Arnold,
but they were not universal. At Eton, early in the eighteenth
century, John Newborough had ruled with Arnold-like
solemnity and sympathy. 'When any hopes of amendment
appeared, he declined severe remedies.' At the same school a
century later, while Keate himself was Lower Master, the
courteous Dr Goodall had been the Upper Master for seven
years. 'There was a pleasant joyousness in him,' says one of
his pupils, 'which beamed and overflowed in his face.' 'A
ripe and excellent scholar and a thorough gentleman, he
commanded on these grounds the entire respect of his pupils,'
says another chronicler. No doubt—and this was indeed the
fault of almost every Master of his day—he was too tolerant
of rowdyism and brutality among the boys, but so was Keate
himself.

Goodall, it is interesting to note, had a profound influence
on his pupil E. C. Hawtrey, who afterwards was under-master
to Keate and followed him as headmaster. It was to Goodall
and not to Keate that Hawtrey turned for inspiration. 'Goodall
caught at the first system of merit and gave it more than its
due praise, but not more than the broken spirit required,' he
wrote. No doubt Keate did not use his battlecry, 'I'll flog you,
sir,' all the time, and it has been maintained that he sometimes
unbent with his senior boys. But his birch was never out of
mind, even if it was occasionally out of sight.

It is not insignificant that when Hawtrey first became head-

Dr Hawtrey

master, the reforms in organisation that he introduced were resented by the boys in the manner that they were accustomed to. There were booings and hootings at 'Absence'; squibs and crackers were let off; masters were mobbed. But as the older boys, brought up under Keate, gradually left, this riotous spirit almost disappeared.

It is an object-lesson in leadership to pass from the bear-garden atmosphere of Keate's Eton, with the spirit of revolt uneasily kept in check by constant flagellation, to the reasonableness of Arnold's Rugby. Keate and Arnold belonged to two different worlds in spirit, but they were not so widely separated in time as is often imagined. Keate was the older man, but their respective headmasterships in fact overlapped. It may well have happened that at the very moment when Keate was attempting to cow his senior pupils into submission, Arnold was talking to *his* seniors as his trusted lieutenants.

'When I have confidence in the Sixth,' he told them, 'there is no post in England I would exchange for this; but if they do not support me, I must go.' Just at the age when they were beginning to feel themselves almost men, and anxious to receive respect, these older boys were offered the confidence and trust of a man they themselves could hardly help respecting. The result was a triumph for Arnold's method as opposed to the method of Keate.

It is not easy to write of Arnold, for so much has already been written. After Thomas Hughes's picturesque eulogy in *Tom Brown's Schooldays* and Dean Stanley's more sober tribute in the *Life of Arnold*, almost the whole English-speaking world for seventy years was persuaded into accepting him as the man who, almost overnight, 'changed the face of education all through the public schools of England.' Such swollen claims invite deflation, and Arnold was clearly a marked man when the intellectuals of the First World War period began sticking their pins into Victorianism.

Fortunately it is no longer necessary to follow Lytton

Strachey, tittering in his beard at the idea that Arnold's legs were shorter than they should have been, and at the fact that Arnold was inclined to be serious over serious things. But without joining the barren band of hero-debunkers, one is still bound to raise an eyebrow at the drastic revolution in education which Arnold is supposed to have brought about in a few years. Educational changes are usually slow, and progress is always uneven.

In a broad sense Arnold did indeed have a very profound effect on public school education, an effect which also filtered through to other types of school. The face of education, however, did not change its expression with quite the rapidity or in quite the way that Arnold's supporters have sometimes implied. We today are so familiar with his name and reputation that we tend to forget that his contemporaries and immediate successors were not equally overawed. Seven or eight years after Arnold had become a headmaster, the great Shrewsbury headmaster, Samuel Butler, could say in all sincerity: 'I don't know what you mean by Arnold's reform of Rugby . . . I know he increased the numbers very much and that they are now considerably on the decline again, but I don't know anything more.' Even at Winchester, Arnold's old school, the Second Master admitted that he had never heard of him until 1838, when Arnold had been ten years at Rugby.

By the time of Arnold's death, four years later, this could hardly have been said. Most people interested in education at least knew his name and a fair number knew he had a reputation as a great educator. But he was far from universally accepted as the great man of English schooling. The educationist R. H. Quick, writing his notable *Essays on Educational Reformers* a quarter of a century after Arnold's death, gives him no more than a passing mention. W. L. Collins (an Etonian) in a well-known book on the public schools published in the same year, is at pains, when dealing with Rugby, to stress how much Arnold owed to previous Rugby headmasters, and how much less his influence on the bulk of his pupils was than 'might be

gathered from some expressions of Dr Arnold's more enthusiastic eulogists.' The rebuke is the more significant because the
writer (unlike certain Wykehamist historians who wished to
prove that Winchester was the fount of all reform) had no axe
to grind, and because he himself greatly admired Arnold.

It is worth noting that Arnold never made exaggerated
claims on his own behalf. Though he found many abuses at
Rugby, as he would have done at any other school, he did not
come to the school in the spirit of a Hercules proposing to clean
out the Augean stables. He was on the whole favourably
impressed with Rugby when he took it over, and records that
he found 'surprisingly few irregularities.' The former headmaster, Dr Wooll, was not remarkable, but he was far from
being the worst of headmasters. Like Keate, he survived more
than one rebellion, and like Keate again, he undertook a mass
flogging on at least one occasion, punishing all the thirty-eight
boys of a class that had given their master the slip, and getting
through the task at the rate of just over a boy a minute. On
the other hand he was no snarler, and his encouragement of
school dramatics—suppressed by many headmasters of his
time—showed an agreeable breadth of mind.

If Arnold did not find Rugby a den of iniquity, nor did he
leave it a paradise. There is a limit to what any headmaster
can achieve in any school. Bullying, drinking, and lawlessness
of other kinds continued throughout his reign. Boys are only
human at any time; and when they are lumped together in a
boarding-school they will often be a good deal less than human.
It is not always recognised that Arnold, who is so often taken
as the supreme representative of the public school system, was
by no means a whole-hearted admirer of it. 'Another system
may be better in itself,' he once said, 'but I am placed in this
system and am bound to try what I can make of it.' He was
always very conscious of the evils that could so easily result
when a large number of boys were left a great deal together,
as the public school system required, and he was never satisfied
that he had found the answer to the problem, in spite of the

hopes he placed in his prefects. 'There had been a system of persecution carried on by the bad against the good,' he cries in a letter written late in his career, 'and then, when complaint was made to me, there came fresh persecution on that very account.' And he speaks, most significantly, of his unwillingness 'to undergo the responsibility of advising any man to send his son to a public school . . . To find this evil thus rife after I have been so many years fighting against it is so sickening that it is very hard not to throw up the cards and upset the table.'

Arnold, then, was by no means the overwhelmingly successful reformer that popular convention has often made him out to be. Yet, when all is said, the popular view of him as a great educational figure, though mistaken in some respects, is true in substance. He tended to overdo the religious and moral pressure; he was not always practical; he lacked humour. But despite these defects, the tremendous force of his personality was thrown so firmly in the right direction—'I believe that boys may be governed a great deal by gentle methods and kindness, if you show that you are not afraid of them'—that he made it easier for such an approach to be followed by later teachers. He invented no new method, but the intensity of his personality gave his methods the stamp of novelty.

His most famous achievement was the development of the prefect system. It was not new in itself, but no headmaster had ever before so impressed upon senior boys how much they were fellow-workers with him in the interests of the school and how much depended on their efforts. Sometimes he expected too much of them; but the sense of responsibility that was given to them showed more unmistakably than it had ever been shown before how seniority in scholars could be a blessing to a school instead of a burden.

Arnold's most significant work, however, was one that has never been fully recognised. It gives him some claim to be considered not only a great headmaster but the first *head*master in English education. He was not merely a guide and captain to his lieutenants, the Sixth Form prefects. He was also the leader of a team of masters; and I think it is true to say that no head-master (so called) had ever been this before. Before his time the more notable headmasters were famous primarily as teachers; after his time headmasters who achieved fame did so as administrators of a school rather than as teachers. That is not entirely a good thing, as some modern headmasters have shown all too clearly, but the development of the headmaster as team-leader was a necessary step in education, and Arnold deserves credit for it.

The independence of the Lower Master has already been shown. As schools grew in size, under-masters often became more numerous; and as the curriculum tended to widen, other masters were appointed to teach the newer subjects. Even so, they remained in a sense outside the school. Their job was to teach, and if they were brought in to help with school discipline it was as a favour to the headmaster rather than as part of their normal school duties. It will be remembered that in the Great Rebellion at Rugby, Dr Ingles was left alone to deal with the rebels because it was a school holiday and there were no masters present. Dr Keate succeeded in checking two rebellions with the aid of his assistant masters, but they had to be called in specially for the purpose. There was no thought that assistant masters ought automatically to be on the spot when trouble was brewing, still less that they were in any way responsible for the tone of the school.

Under Dr Arnold, assistant masters became vital to the good order of the school. He increased the salaries of the staff, thereby making it unnecessary for them to devote half their attention to local curacies and the like, and he made a practice of putting the old Dames' boarding-houses under the exclusive care of individual masters. Even more important than this was his deliberate practice of consulting his staff on all matters of school discipline. Every three weeks he held a council of masters to discuss school matters, at which every master was free to express an opinion, and at which every opinion was

courteously considered. So long as no fundamental principle
was contradicted, he was prepared to accept a majority vote
against his own suggestions.

Present-day masters with a keen recollection of wasted
hours spent in discussing nothing at great length may feel that
the introduction of staff meetings was an innovation of doubtful benefit. But the value of a new measure must be judged by
its original quality, not by subsequent perversions of it, and
the three-weekly masters' meetings called by Arnold did more
than anything else to make it clear, once and for all, that in
matters of school discipline a master at a public grammar
school was a member of a team and not just an interested
spectator.

'Nothing delights me more,' Arnold said of one of his
colleagues, 'than to think that boys are sent here for his sake
rather than for mine.' His eagerness to obtain first-class assistants,
and his readiness to share credit with them, was one reason
why Arnold's approach to education spread from Rugby
to other schools. Men who had taught under him, and profited
by the contact, instinctively carried on his work when they
were appointed as headmasters to other schools. Some of
his senior pupils, too, who had shared an almost equally close
co-operation with him, also acted as his apostles when they,
in turn, entered the teaching profession and became headmasters; and so the spirit of Arnold spread in some degree
from school to school during the nineteenth century.

An interesting feature of Arnold's influence is the number
of his disciples who were chosen to take charge of the new
public schools which were springing up like daisies on a
lawn during the 1850's and 1860's. Marlborough, Wellington,
Haileybury, and Clifton all turned to Rugby for leadership.
Cotton, Benson, A. G. Butler, and Percival all became notable
headmasters. Even one of the old schools, Harrow, when it
was in the depths, looked to an old Rugbeian to save it.

C. J. Vaughan, who rescued Harrow, and George Cotton,

the saviour of Marlborough, are particularly interesting examples of Arnold's influence, because the results of their work were so striking. They were more definitely reformers than Arnold ever was, because the schools to which they were appointed were far more in need of reform than the Rugby of 1828.

C. J. Vaughan was the first and more famous. He came to Harrow in 1844 when the Red Nightcap Club was in its prime, and drunkenness, dissipation, and bullying were at their height. The Rev. Christopher Wordsworth, one of the poet's nephews, had been headmaster for eight years, and had left it to the prefects to take care of the social life of the school. As he unfortunately lacked the ability to inspire them, they carried out their work in the way that best suited their personal tastes, and the school's reputation became such that the numbers sank as low as 69.

Vaughan not only realised the importance of giving prefects a real sense of responsibility. He also had the ability to make his prefects realise it too, and he possessed a tact and personal charm that enabled him to introduce reforms into an old school without alienating its pupils. Even Guy Fawkes night was tamed without causing a riot.

Vaughan achieved a good deal, and brought the school's numbers up from 69 to 438. But a rise in the school population is by no means an infallible test of a headmaster's greatness (Arnold laid stress on *limiting* the numbers at Rugby), and it would be easy to exaggerate Vaughan's success. Though he inspired his prefects in a way that his immediate predecessors had been unable to do, he did not fully convert them, and he tended to over-estimate their importance. Himself one of Arnold's most able and trusted lieutenants, he failed to appreciate that prefects are still boys, with all the lack of judgment and experience which necessarily limits the wisdom even of the older boys. The supervision of boys by masters he regarded as 'spying,' and his prefects were actually forbidden to refer problems to himself except for 'grave moral offences.' As he also gave them the power to inflict corporal punishment, he opened the door to abuses that were almost as bad as those he had set out to cure. The results were less satisfactory than at Rugby, and even here they were far from perfect.

Arnold's success, moreover, had rested even more upon his relations with his staff than upon his reliance on his prefects. This was something that Vaughan, an ex-prefect, failed to appreciate. His own relations with the Harrow staff were never very satisfactory. He was more of a favourite with the boys than with the masters—always an unfortunate situation for a headmaster to be in.

No doubt the masters themselves were not a little at fault: they seem to have been a pretty uninspiring lot. But perhaps they were not always to blame.

A boy called Dodd was once sent to Vaughan for punishment. The headmaster asked him his name, started to write it down, and then stopped.

'Do you spell it with one *d* or two?'

'Three, sir,' replied the boy.

The headmaster burst out laughing and dismissed the boy without punishment.

'I could no more have punished that boy,' he afterwards said, 'than I could have flown. Nobody before ever gave me such a lesson in spelling.'

The incident does credit to Vaughan's sense of humour, but perhaps it indicates one reason why his popularity was greater with the boys than with the staff.

A later Harrow headmaster, Dr Joseph Wood, suffered from the same weakness. He used to select certain sixth form boys, let them off some of their ordinary work, to the disadvantage and annoyance of their form master, and get them to come to his study two or three evenings a week to read the Iliad, seated in comfortable armchairs round the fireside. Then they would have cake and claret, and he would frequently keep them talking till past 10.30 p.m. against a strict house rule, thereby annoying their housemasters. It was Dr Wood (when he was headmaster of Tonbridge) who, noting that a boy's housemaster had written on his school report 'I fear he does not always do his best,' added in the adjacent headmaster's space, '*Neither do I. J.W.*'

This sort of thing reveals humour and a sense of proportion, but it also shows a dangerous tendency to court popularity at the expense of the assistant masters. The good headmaster must at all costs resist the temptation, for it is an insidious evil which can ruin the spirit of a school.

George Cotton was no seeker of popularity, though he was a popular headmaster. He is perhaps the least known of the great headmasters; but it would hardly be exaggerating to say that he is in many ways the most unquestionably great. When he went to Marlborough in 1851 he found it, eight years after it had been launched, nothing but a floating wreck. The Rev. Mr Wilkinson, as we saw in Chapter Four, had left the school in a state of chaotic disorder, the senseless system of chronic flogging having broken down before the spirit of mutiny.

Mr Cotton was a man who could talk to boys on their own level without pandering to their weaknesses. The young master who discusses cricket and work with Tom and Arthur in the penultimate chapter of *Tom Brown's Schooldays* was none other than the future headmaster of Marlborough, 'a tall, slight, and rather gaunt man, with a bushy eyebrow, and a dry humorous smile.'

Though his personality was very much his own, he had learnt more from Arnold than any other Rugby master or boy had done. Three things in particular he brought with him from the Midlands. One was the ability to talk frankly to boys; another was an understanding of how prefects could be used to give tone to the school; and a third was the realisation that the spirit of a school depended very much on the spirit of the staff. Moreover, though no gamesman himself ('I don't understand cricket,' he admits to Tom Brown), he saw that organised games were the solution to the indiscipline of riotous Marlborough, and he became the first headmaster to make the playing-field the centre of a school's activity. If public schools in a later age carried the cult of athleticism to excess, and based their prefect system on the cult, that is no fault of Cotton's.

More than any headmaster before him, and a great many after him, Cotton was intensely aware of the importance of having the right men on the staff. Within two or three years almost all Mr Wilkinson's dreary floggers had disappeared. They were replaced by young and enthusiastic men who, in contrast to their predecessors, had some natural liking for boys.

Mr Cotton's reforms were not carried out in a flash. They were handicapped, moreover, by constant financial crises. Throughout his headmastership the school was so hard pressed for money that it was often doubtful whether it would be able to carry on, and impossible to pay the staff an adequate salary. Yet there was no mistaking the change that came over the school within a few years. When Mr Cotton arrived, there was hardly a worse school to be found anywhere; when he left, only six years later, Marlborough was one of the best schools in England.

If that does not reveal true greatness in a headmaster, I do not know what does.

Men of the same reforming character have, of course, appeared in many different types of school. At the Westcott Street Board School in Southwark, for instance, the children in the eighteen-seventies used to offer the excuse, 'Gone out nicking (i.e. thieving),' as a normal excuse for absence, and teachers were so often mobbed on their way from school that they had to leave the building in a body, and sometimes sought police protection. Within a few years the whole atmosphere was changed, largely by the influence exercised by a new headmaster, 'as true a missionary,' said one of H.M. Inspectors, 'as ever sailed from our shores to spend his life among savages.'

There is an old aphorism, said to have originated at Rugby,

which lays down that if a headmaster can neither teach, nor preach, nor organise, then he ought to be either a scholar or a gentleman.

Dr Longley, at Harrow in 1830, was undistinguished in the first four capacities. The boys, moreover, tricked him as they pleased. A pupil one day had the effrontery to steal all the meat from a pie that the Doctor was offering to some guests, leaving only the crust. His only comment, when the boy owned up, was: 'I am glad you told me.' Yet, although he had little influence on his pupils, he squeezes into the ranks of legitimate headmasters on the fifth count. The boys tricked him but they liked him too; and no kindlier epitaph has been written on any headmaster then Anthony Trollope's comment that 'Dr Longley never in his life was able to say an ill-natured word.'

Here he differed not only from the more efficient Dr George Butler, with whom Trollope was making comparison, but with a good many other Heads—such as the headmaster of Bromsgrove School, whom Laurence Housman 'feared more than I have feared any other person before or since.' When he caned anyone, said Housman, he had an infuriated manner which was terrifying in its effect and evil in its spirit; and he was as liable to cane a boy for a timid effort to please as for deliberate wrong-doing. He openly sneered at the shabby clothes in which Housman, as a small boy, was sent to school by his parents. Snobbishly disliking the day boys, sons of tradesmen, who lowered the school tone, as he thought, by their presence, he used to call them by the insulting nicknames used by the boarders—'Bacon' was the grocer's son and 'Cart-horse' the farmer's. When the day boys beat the lower boarding school at football the headmaster was so incensed that he ordered a return match to be played immediately.

Most headmasters, fortunately, are less unpleasant than this in their attitude to their pupils. Officiousness is commoner than offensiveness, and more headmasters are odd than odious.

Such, for example, was Dr Saunders, of Charterhouse,

whose pronunciation was so peculiar that boys often did not know to whom he was referring. He called up a pupil one day in class, tapped a letter that he held in his hand, and said sympathetically: 'I am sorry to tell you that your aunt is dead.'

'But, sir,' replied the boy, 'I haven't got an aunt!'

Instead of jumping to the obvious conclusion that he had called the wrong boy, he merely cried, 'Foolish fellow!' and boxed the boy's ears.

Moss of Shrewsbury may perhaps be included among the peculiar headmasters in regard to sport. His ignorance was bottomless. 'What time do they draw stumps?' he is said to have asked at a football match; and when it was reported to him that a member of a shooting eight had hit the bull five times he exclaimed indignantly: 'Then I hope due remuneration will be paid to the owner of the unfortunate animal.' Though not a violent man he once administered eighty-eight strokes with the birch to a pupil, which he (and strangely enough the Head of the School also) maintained was not excessive. When he retired he went to live, appropriately, at a place named Much Birch.

Almond of Loretto, distinguished pioneer though he was in certain aspects of physical education, was also rather strange in his habits. His fetishes were fresh air, freedom, and frankness, and he gave his pupils all three. His classroom windows were always open, even in winter. His pupils went where they wished and wore what they pleased as long as it was not too formal, while he himself strode about in a grey flannel shirt and trousers, on occasions with a pair of red braces hanging down behind. He encouraged his pupils to offer their views on the running of the school, which may be a good thing; and he discussed the merits and demerits of his staff with the boys, which is definitely a bad thing. Not surprisingly, some of his masters left without any affection for Loretto. Finally, when a headmaster of over forty, about to set out to propose to a young lady of twenty, begins by talking over the affair with his head prefect, we may reasonably feel that frankness is being carried to almost unhealthy lengths.

The temptation to go on writing about headmasters, individually or as types, must be resisted. There have been really good ones, such as Arnold and Cotton, and definitely bad ones, such as the Rev. James Atcherley, Samuel Butler's immediate predecessor at Shrewsbury, whose favourite pastime was to compete with the second master in kicking at a flitch of bacon hung from the kitchen ceiling, and who gave away and mutilated the books in the school library. Most headmasters have been somewhere in between.

Is there a characteristic headmasterly quality? Generalisations are unsafe; but perhaps it is not too far from the truth to suggest that if there is such a quality, it is an unwillingness to be committed to anything. The Rev J. Branthwaite of St Nicholas College, Shoreham, typified the trait.

'When he was asked by a boy for leave to do something out of the ordinary he weighed the pros and balanced the cons, and after long indecision finally gave so modified a permission that the boys described the answer as "Yes, only no." '

In similar spirit Dr Selwyn, twenty years headmaster of Uppingham, when pressed by four boys for permission to go and skate on a frozen lake some way from the school, at length reluctantly gave a kind of assent.

'Well, two of you may go,' he conceded.

Two of them went, got into some small difficulty, and were interviewed by the headmaster on their return. Eager to disclaim all responsibility for the trouble, he insisted that they had gone without his permission.

'But, sir,' protested the boys, 'you said two of us could go.'

'Ah yes,' Dr Selwyn replied hastily, 'but I didn't say *which* two.'

CHAPTER SEVEN

ONCE MORE UNTO THE BREECH

IN a dialogue exercise contained in an old Latin text-book, written over a thousand years ago, the pupils (rather improbably) beg the master to teach them to speak Latin correctly.

'Are you prepared to be flogged in the course of your learning?' the master asks.

'We would rather be flogged,' reply the pupils (even more improbably), 'than remain ignorant.'

The book, being written by a teacher, reflects medieval education from the master's angle rather than from the pupil's. But even though the author may be putting into the mouths of his pupils opinions which they never held, at the same time he reveals two important facts about the teaching of his day. The masters regarded Latin as the root of all education, and they believed that the natural way of teaching it was to drive it upwards from seat to cerebrum.

For nearly a thousand years teaching method on these points contrived to remain stationary. The chief matter of learning was Latin, and the key to the teaching of it was the birch.

So closely linked in official eyes was the profession of schoolmastering with the practice of flogging, that it was not uncommon for a master on being appointed, or even on receiving his degree, to be formally presented with a rod, birch, or other implement as the symbol of his office.

Certainly he rarely failed to use it. By the sixteenth century, when schools were growing bigger and more numerous, the swish of the birch must have been one of the most familiar sounds in the country.

It is sometimes said, both by opponents of corporal punishment and by its approvers, that boys do not really mind it. That may be true, or partly true, of the discreet one-on-each-hand caning dubiously administered by modern schoolmasters with one eye on the law. It was not so true of the old-time flogging. It may seem strange to blasé Etonians of today to think that a public schoolboy should run away to avoid being caned. Yet that is what Eton boys were known to do in Elizabeth's reign, and what is more, the greatest statesman of the day gave them his sympathy.

'I have strange news brought me,' said Lord Burghley, 'that divers scholars of Eton be run away from the school for fear of a beating.' And he added, 'I wish some more discretion were in many schoolmasters, in using correction, than commonly there is, who many times punish rather the weakness of nature than the fault of the scholar.'

The backward boy in the sixteenth century was not the privileged person that he has since become. 'The misery I had at the Grammar School,' complained a former pupil of St Paul's School, 'was very great by reason of my inaptness. The master (Dr Cook) with lashes set more than seven scars on my hide, which yet remain.' And it was said of Richard Neile, who was at Westminster in the fifteen-seventies: 'The schoolmaster was never off his breech.' The result was not to brighten his wits but to make him 'so verie a dunce that he could never make a correct Latin theme'—a limitation which, however, did not prevent him from subsequently becoming an Archbishop.

Masters were rarely put off by the failure of the rod to turn a dullard into a genius, or by the fact that it might frighten talent away. A good thrashing was the accepted method of teaching Latin, and schoolmasters, like the members of other professions and trades, tended to be conservative in their ways. Some of them persuaded themselves (and even their pupils) that they were doing their victims a good turn.

'This I do to save you from the gallows,' Johnson's master

used to say as he flogged his pupils unmercifully for classical ignorance; and Johnson was so far convinced as to state in after years: 'My master whipt me very well. Without that, Sir, I should have done nothing.'

Want of knowledge was not, of course, the only fault to be punished by flogging. For many centuries the birch was the answer to almost every misdemeanour. Even prefects were not always immune. The Westminster Statutes of 1560, for instance, laid it down that 'if any monitor commits an offence or neglects to perform his duty he shall be severely flogged as an example to others.'

Worst of all offences, from the master's point of view, was that of running away, which implied both a criticism of the school and a vague threat to the master's continuity of employment. This was something that must be nipped in the bud; and the birch was hastily brought into action. Thus a boy whose life in a boarding-school was made so wretched, by the masters or by his school-fellows, or by both, that he could endure it no longer and sought refuge in flight, was invariably, on his returning, given a severe public thrashing to convince him that school was after all quite a desirable place.

Late in the eighteen-fifties, for example, a new boy arrived at Lancing College, and after a week of it ran away. A few days later he was brought back by his guardians. Though he tried to show a pride in his school by politely showing them over it he was automatically given a public birching the same evening. Still unconvinced that he was happy at school, he bolted again after a few more days. This time he wisely avoided his guardians' company, but they engaged detectives to find him and he was caught after ten days. Once again he was flogged before the whole school. He remained obstinately discontented with school life; and although locked up in a room in the headmaster's house, he escaped and ran away to sea.

But no runaways were quite so harshly treated as the Blue-coat boys who turned their backs on the charity dispensed at

Christ's Hospital. Readers of Elia's *Essays* will recall the treatment meted out in Lamb's early days.

'The sight of a boy in fetters, upon the day of my first putting on the blue clothes, was not exactly fitted to assuage the natural terrors of initiation . . . I was told he had *run away*. This was the punishment for the first offence.—As a novice, I was soon after taken to see the dungeons. These were little square Bedlam cells, where a boy could just lie at his length upon straw and a blanket—a mattress, I think, was afterwards substituted—with a peep of light let in askance from a prison orifice at top, barely enough to read by. Here the poor boy was locked in by himself all day, without sight of any but the porter who brought him his bread and water—who *might not speak to him*—or of the beadle, who came twice a week to call him out to receive his periodical chastisement . . . and here he was shut up by himself *of nights*, out of the reach of any sound.'

That was the punishment for the second offence. Any boy who was so bold or so desperate as to abscond a third time from Newgate Street was brought back only to be publicly driven out, after a long and public scourging round the hall. 'We were generally too faint with attending to the previous *disgusting circumstances* to make accurate report with our eyes of the degree of corporal suffering inflicted. Report, of course, gave out the back knotty and livid.'

Report did not err, nor was Lamb romancing. Christ's Hospital was notorious for the brutality of its floggings, and retained this sinister reputation long after a good many schools had experienced some humanising influences.

The girls and young bluecoat boys had been removed from the London hospital to Hertford in the eighteenth century, but the boys do not seem to have fared much better. A boy who was there from 1825 to 1832 described in later years how impressed he was on his first day by the fear inspired by the headmaster. The cane was constantly in use in the schoolroom; and in due course the birch was brought into action.

'At length I was startled by his sonorous voice uttering, in a tone of thunder, those words of terror to every Blue, "Go you there! Get me a birch-rod!"—pointing at the same time with his finger to a door leading from the school into the backyard, forming, in consequence of double doors, a small lobby.' The lobby was so narrow that the flogger had to stand on the step, and 'the inclination of the body towards the door caused it to open every time the arm struck, while the shrieks of the sufferer met the ear.' The new boy was equally impressed by the pale faces of his fellow pupils, 'terrified by the fate of their companions.'

Well might faces be pale at the Bluecoat schools, which distinguished themselves from more enlightened places of learning by commonly handing over the severest form of punishment to the coarse hands of the beadles, rough men with no spark of refinement. They carried out their gross task in the grossest way, without any regard to the character of the victim or the nature of his offence.

A most respectable clergyman, the Rev. Andrew Drew, M.A., describes the scene as it was enacted in the eighteen-forties, sixty years after Lamb's schooldays.

'Two men are required for the operation. One takes hold of the boy, hoists him on his back by the wrists, and keeps him suspended. The other strips off his coat, and armed with a large and heavy rod, gives fifteen cuts on the boy's bare back, and these with might and main.

'This, however, was a mild flogging, for if the offence was at all great the boy received fifteen more in another place with a fresh rod; and that, at least in my time, used to be the punishment for running away. I have seen a large and powerful man, one of the beadles, split his own shirt-sleeve right down with the violence he used in flogging a poor little lad of thirteen.'

Even innocence was of no avail.

'As long as I live,' wrote Mr Drew, 'I shall never forget a scene that I once witnessed. A small and delicate lad, by name

of Blount, slept in the bed next to me. A big boy had compelled
Blount to go and bring him some lumps of sugar out of the
monitors' sugar-basin. The big boy ate the sugar himself and
the small boy had none of it. The facts of the case became known
to the monitor, who reported it to the Steward, who directed
Blount to be flogged as a thief and did not punish the big boy.

'That night poor little Blount could not sleep, and at last
he begged me to help him. I accordingly took his shirt off,
and found his back, from the shoulders down to the waist, one
mass of lacerated flesh, the blood sticking to his shirt so as to
cause agony in getting it off. I then, with my finger and thumb,
pulled out of his back at least a dozen pieces of birch-rod,
which had penetrated deep into the flesh. That boy's back
looked more like a piece of raw meat than anything else.'

Such an act of criminal injustice, one hopes—without complete conviction—may have been comparatively rare. But
the method of assault was certainly not unexampled at either
of the Bluecoat schools. As late as the 1870's a boy at the
Hertford school, so an old Blue recorded, was flogged in the
traditional manner.

'He was hoisted by one beadle, and another birched him,
his back being raw for some days afterwards; and the agony he
endured at night, when he took off his shirt, was fearful, as
the shirt stuck to his back, clotted with blood. The boy was
then under twelve years of age.'

Christ's Hospital has the blackest record for official brutality,
but it is by no means alone, even in the period following
Arnold's death. No one who has read the preceding chapters
will be surprised to learn that Marlborough's first decade was
disgraced by the savagery of its incompetent staff.

'A village schoolmaster nowadays,' said Edward Lockwood
in the 'nineties, 'would, I am glad to say, get a month at the
treadmill if he beat a boy as I was beaten at school. When, on
my arrival home, I was undressed and put to bed by my
tender-hearted nurse, she viewed my back with the utmost
horror and indignation.'

The nurse, one fears, cannot have been a truly religious woman to allow her sympathy to get so out of hand. Lockwood's father, a devout clergyman, reproved her, explaining that as the punishment had been administered by men called to the ministry of God, the victim must have deserved every blow he received.

His offence was, in fact, the familiar one of failing to learn Latin, which, in the complete absence of any actual teaching, this particular small boy entirely failed to understand. As soon as he returned to school, his master again 'proceeded to apply his cane to my back, which had hardly healed from the bruises it had received before . . . I had not the faintest idea what the Latin grammar was all about, and as no one made the faintest attempt to explain anything, I gave up all hope of understanding it.'

This was not an exceptional instance. One of the earliest senior boys of the school—one who had more good to say of it than any other of its original pupils—strongly excepted from his praise the violent and constant canings in which the staff indulged. 'The word "brutal," ' he considered, 'is the only one that meets the case.' One reverend master, it is recorded in the School's official history, lost complete control of himself in attempting to make a stoical pupil cry out with pain. In the end he had to give up, exhausted, without success. His victim was taken off to the sick-room, where strips of his shirt were extracted from his lacerated back.

It is not surprising that a number of boys failed to appreciate the kind of education given at this school in its first years, and ran away. Not only were they caught, brought back, and severely flogged, but, as a further discouragement to flight, the whole form was punished if any boy in it tried to escape from the school.

For our final episode in scholastic desertion we must return to the Christ's Hospital of 1877, in which year a pupil named William Gibbs was in trouble with the authorities. He was one of forty boys who had been sent, about the age of twelve or thirteen, from Hertford to the main school in London. He came with varied reports. The writing master found him 'obliging and good-natured,' but the Steward reported his character as 'very indifferent'; which may perhaps tell us more about the men than about the boy.

On June 23 he was caned for gross insolence to the drill master. After the punishment he ran home (for many of the Bluecoat boarders had families in London), explaining to his parents that he had a half-holiday. He told his sister, however, that he had been cruelly treated at school. He was taken back to school next day, and received the usual public flogging for desertion.

A week later he was in trouble again, being slapped by a monitor for scuffling during a scripture lesson. The monitor also warned him that he would be reported to the headmaster. It seemed likely that another flogging was coming to him, so once more he ran away, staying out all night. When the following day he went home, he told his family that he was being bullied by the monitor, a statement which may have had some element of truth in it or which was possibly merely an excuse to cover his flight and to avoid being sent back. 'If I'm put under that monitor again I'll hang myself,' he threatened.

None the less his father and a friend of the family took him back, and though he seemed afraid of being punished they would not let him run away. The delinquent was placed in a ward by himself, watched over by the head nurse of the wards. 'He looked defiant,' she said, and added: 'He looked as if he did not care much what happened.' He was left alone to contemplate his future flogging.

The head nurse was apparently a bad judge of character, for the defiant pupil, indifferent to his coming punishment, was found, two hours later, hanging from the ventilator with a cord round his neck, stone dead.

Even at Christ's Hospital this was felt to be rather an extreme measure; and in the world outside Newgate Street it caused a stir. Some frank opinions were expressed; and although various Old Blues rushed forward to defend the indefensible, others, among them men of educational standing, spoke out boldly.

'When I see how happy small boys can be made at school,' said the headmaster of Blundell's School, 'I feel a deep regret, which my love and gratitude towards my old school only makes the more bitter, at the thought of the tears needlessly shed there each day.'

'I can vouch absolutely,' stated A. J. Butler, a master at Winchester College, 'for the fact that, in my time at Christ's Hospital (eight years ago), the punishments were often very cruel and revolting.'

'As regards the education given,' the Vicar of St Antholin's, Nunhead, recorded in *The Times*, 'I believe that Christ's Hospital is second to no school in England; but when I have said that I have said all in its praise. I can only add that the seven years I spent in that school were years of misery and suffering. Nothing in this world would induce me to send one of my sons to the same school.'

An official inquiry was ordered by the Home Secretary.

The Report, when it appeared, was politely vague, its authors being anxious to avoid blaming anybody but the victim. No doubt Gibbs was an unsatisfactory pupil in many ways, possibly stubborn, perhaps of rather low intelligence. The Report described him as a bully; though later, several boys told his father that he had *protected* them from bullying. An earlier teacher reported that he had found Gibbs 'tractable and teachable.' 'You may bend him,' he added, 'but you will not break him.' The Report curiously contrived to change this plain statement into its opposite, thereby implying that breaking was the treatment recommended even by earlier teachers. A public correction of the error was given to the Press by the teacher concerned; and the blunder does not leave us with much confidence in the Report.

Anyhow, Christ's Hospital had broken William Gibbs, and

was now eager to forget about him as quickly as possible; which it did so effectively that he is not even mentioned in the histories of the school.

It would, of course, be absurd to suggest that floggings in the old days were usually fatal. They were often unduly severe and too often undeserved, but the victims survived them. None the less, the birch-rod and the cane occupied, as we have already seen, a very prominent place in school. Details concerning their construction and use appear quite freely in old school statutes and educational treatises.

'A good sharp birchen rod and free from knots, for willow wands are insufferable' is the opinion of Charles Hoole in the mid-seventeenth century. Earlier, John Brinsley had suggested 'a small red willow where birch cannot be had.' At Charterhouse, as at many other schools, the implement was a five-foot bunch of birch switches, fastened at the handle end, and 'armed with buds as big as thorns, renewed after six strokes for fresh excoriation,' so an early nineteenth century pupil tells us. At Winchester, for many years, instead of a birch, four long and flexible apple twigs were used, fastened into grooves in a two-foot handle. But the more customary birch was substituted in the eighteen-sixties.

Private schools and village schools were no less ready than public schools to employ these instruments. Southey, indeed, suggests that punishments at the end of the eighteenth century were nearly always more severe in private schools than in public ones; though, ironically, at his own private school there was only one flogging (carried out with 'a scourge of pack-thread instead of a rod'), while he himself was expelled from Westminster for condemning the headmaster's free use of the birch. Dickens certainly endured as much pain from Mr Jones at Wellington House Academy as Thackeray from Dr Russell at Charterhouse, where 'little boys [were] flogged into a premature Hades.' A. F. Leach, ex-pupil and historian of Winchester College, found Dr Moberly far less severe than

Dr Dyne of Cholmely School, Highgate, and, moreover, at Winchester 'never had to endure the butt-end of the birch on the palm of the hand when saying a lesson, for any and every mistake, an abominable practice which Dr Dyne loved.'

George Tomlinson, a Labour Minister of Education, who attended the Rishton Wesleyan School, Lancs., at the very end of the last century, 'was thrashed in every room of that school. For particularly serious crimes I was taken into the Minister's Vestry and thrashed there.'

No doubt both private and village schools varied more in their methods than public schools, where traditional practices are apt to become fixed. Not one of the semi-fictitious dames in Mary Russell Mitford's village school had recourse to willow, birch, or strap, but Shenstone did not draw entirely on his imagination in his portraiture of the schoolmistress 'who boasts unruly brats with birch to tame'—though it may be that birch trees did not always grow so conveniently near the village school as his poem suggests.

In some schools it was the practice to set aside a certain day—usually Friday—for the corporal punishment of offenders during the week. Thus it was at Eton in the sixteenth century, and thus again at Winchester in the seventeenth.

'Bloody Friday comes next, and I say bloody, because if you have sinned during the week, you will suffer cruel pain. Down on your knees, and two boys, duly summoned, will loose your braces and let down your breeches.'

John Brinsley, the comparatively humane master of the grammar school at Ashby-de-la-Zouch in Shakespeare's day, was not in favour of having a fixed flogging day 'lest keeping a set time, any absent themselves by feigned excuses or otherwise, or cry unto their parents that they dare not go to the school because they must be beaten.' The parents of Ashby in this supposedly rough and brutal century must have been more tender-hearted than those of Gibbs and Lockwood in the days of Queen Victoria. But it may have been that Brinsley was just being unduly cautious. He was the type of teacher who likes to do everything according to the book, and his whole system of education was worked out to cover every contingency. Had he lived in modern times his register would always have been closed on the dot, his mark book invariably up to date, and his scheme of work and lesson notes ready for inspection at a moment's notice.

On the subject of corporal punishment he was precise in every particular—and, to do him justice, quite reasonable. Flogging was the last resort, but it was necessary when a boy was defiant or stubborn, lest his actions should influence the other boys.

The main thing was to make sure of holding the boy firmly, 'so as he cannot anyway hurt himself or others, be he never so peevish.' Three or four strong and amenable pupils were appointed to seize the victim and hold him over a form or better still to a post, 'so that he cannot stir hand nor foot.' After the flogging the victim must not be allowed to go away 'murmuring, pouting, or blowing and puffing.' Still less may he be allowed to avoid punishment by wriggling away, or on the next occasion correction will be doubly difficult.

In the more famous schools flogging became so much an accepted part of school routine that it was hardly necessary to have the victim held down. None the less the practice of getting other boys to assist in the execution remained a common one. At Westminster, for instance, the victim was hoisted on the back of another boy, a method employed by Dr Busby and lasting till well into the nineteenth century. 'This is certainly the most unpleasant form of flogging at Westminster,' a senior pupil of the eighteen-eighties records. At Eton a praepostor was always present, whose duty was to hand the birches to the headmaster: each offender had a birch to himself, for which he was privileged to pay. The victim knelt over a flogging-block, while two holders-down stood behind him, though their office, at least in later years, was not to hold down the offender but to hold up his shirt. These at one time were always junior collegers, a fact which, as a writer of the 'sixties

Discipline in Dickens's days

pointed out, did not tend to improve relations between college boys and oppidans.

At Winchester in the seventeenth century, two boys were summoned to unfasten the culprit's braces and lower his breeches. By the eighteenth century it had become traditional at Winchester to flog not the buttocks but the small of the back, the shirt and waistcoat being held up for the purpose. By the same period Friday was ceasing to have its former bloody significance, and the penalty usually came on the day after the sentence. Occasionally a victim guilty of a fault deemed particularly disgraceful had to stand on a form close to the place of execution to meditate, in full view of the school, on what was coming to him. This was known as 'standing under the nail,' the 'nail,' in fact, being the socket for a candle-sconce.

How effective, one naturally wonders, were these floggings?

Of course there can be no simple answer. Effectiveness depended on the severity of the flogging, the type of offence —if, indeed, there was an offence—the attitude of the flogger, the character of the victim, and the rarity or familiarity of the occasion.

First-hand evidence is always worth more than generalisation, so let us have the impressions of some pupils of the eighteen-seventies who watched or endured these old flogging ceremonies.

'When I first came to Eton and was told how culprits were dealt with, I fancied I was being hoaxed,' said Brinsley Richards. 'I never quite believed the stories I heard until I actually saw a boy flogged, and I can never forget the impression which the sight produced upon me . . . Several dozens of fellows clambered upon forms and desks to see Neville corrected, and I got a front place, my heart thumping and seeming to make great leaps within me. Next moment, when he knelt on the step of the block and when the Lower Master inflicted upon his person

six cuts that sounded like the splashings of so many buckets of
water, I turned almost faint.'

And this is how it seemed to a victim of the Lower Master
in the same school:

'After fumbling over several brace buttons you took your
station on the block, while two acolyte "Tugs" held up your
shirt, then you crammed a handkerchief into your mouth
with one hand and held the other straight down, protected
with starched cuff, to prevent the ends of the birch from curling
round your body. This the old man always resented as baulking
him of his due. "He-he! very idle boy, take your hand away";
a command which, when disobeyed, resulted in ten or fourteen
cuts, a matter ascertained by the knowing ones to be preferable
to the usual unprotected six strokes . . . And you went away,
smarting as much from the indignity as from the pain, and
vowing that you would rather write out endless impositions
than let it occur again.'

The master's approach to the ceremony varied even more
than the victim's. 'I knew one master,' said Henry Peacham,
'who in winter would ordinarily on a cold morning whip his
boys for no other purpose than to get himself in a heat:
another beat them for swearing, and all the while swears
himself with horrible oaths.' Men such as Udall and Boyer
were obviously sadists.

The latter, as Charles Lamb tells us, used sometimes to
seek entertainment in his floggings when he was in one of his
gentler moods. Between each paragraph of the Latin prose that
he was reading with his class he would administer a stroke with
his birch. In the same spirit a master at Hastings Grammar
School in the 'eighties used to thrash his pupils with great
gusto, pausing after each stroke to offer rough witticisms.
'Did it hurt much? Rub it in! Rub it in! We'll try another
presently.' (In due course this master took Holy Orders.)

Richard Mulcaster, another sadist, was once caught out
when, unusually, he attempted to bring a note of facetiousness
into his flogging. A boy was ready one day for execution,

F

kneeling for punishment with his breeches down. 'Out of his insulting humour the master stood pausing awhile over his breech; and there a merry conceit taking him he said, "I ask ye banns of Matrimony between this boy's buttocks of such a parish on ye one side and Lady Birch of this parish on ye other side; and if any man can show any lawful cause why they should not be joined together let him speak, for this is ye last time of asking." '

Such pedagogic jests are merely rhetorical in intention, and Mulcaster must have been a good deal surprised when a bold boy stood up and said, 'Master, I forbid the banns.'

'Yea sirrah, and why so?' the master demanded ominously.

'Because all parties are not agreed,' the boy answered promptly.

It is at least to Mulcaster's credit that—if the account is true—he 'spared the one's fault and the other's presumption.'

Even Keate was known on occasions to spare a victim. A boy who was due for punishment and was very nervous about it was advised by some mischievous companions to apply a preparation of gall to his seat, thus, they assured him, making it impervious to pain. He gullibly followed the direction, ignorant of the fact that gall is one of the chief ingredients of writing-ink. Fortunately for himself he discovered the result before the time for execution came. The idea of presenting an ink-blackened backside to the irascible Dr Keate terrified him. He explained the situation to his tutor, and the headmaster, taken in a good mood, agreed that a flogging in the circumstances, would lose its impressiveness. He changed the punishment to an imposition and did not even flog the mischievous advisers.

One of the absurdities of the flogging convention was the capriciousness with which it was administered. It did not necessarily happen that a bad boy was the victim, nor were virtue and ability necessarily a safeguard. Even though the bestial injustice offered to young Blount at Christ's Hospital may have been exceptional, the armour of righteousness had its chinks in most schools. Thus at Harrow, in Dr George Butler's time, a clever boy (Walter Trevelyan), frequently commended by the master, was flogged twice in six weeks for not knowing his lessons perfectly, whereas a boy who took a leading part in breaking school rules and following cruel customs escaped without any flogging at all. Anthony Trollope, a wretched, bullied, dirty child of seven, the youngest boy in the school, was frequently flogged by the august headmaster.

One of the most curious ways of inviting Fortune to hold the birch rod was a practice of the headmaster of Winchester. In the huge schoolroom three or four forms might all be preparing lessons. Only half a dozen boys were allowed to leave the room, for the usual purpose, at any one time. Sometimes, when the master's attention was elsewhere, other boys would slip out without permission.

On a fine summer afternoon the headmaster, busy with his seniors, might look up from his high throne and notice that the rest of the schoolroom had rather a deserted appearance. He would send out a couple of prefects to search the playing-fields. In due course a herd of truants would be driven in. Instead of giving them all extra work, Dr Moberly had recourse to the inevitable birch. But to flog the lot would be too time-wasting and burdensome, he felt; so the offenders were made to 'cut in a book.' This meant that a certain letter in a particular book was chosen at random (for example the first letter in the fourth line). Then every boy in turn was called up to turn a page in the book. The half-dozen or so pupils who turned to a page on which the first letter in the fourth line was an *a*, or nearest to an *a*, were selected for punishment, and the rest were allowed to escape.

In such situations it becomes almost inevitable that the penalty loses something of the impressive effect that it ought to have if it is to be employed at all. Indeed, a former pupil of Moberly's has recorded that a birching of two cribbers, to which the whole form was invited, 'was regarded as a good joke by the rest of us.'

When flogging becomes farcical it is obviously time to drop it. The over-free use of the birch made education ridiculous as well as ferocious, and during this century floggings and canings have grown steadily less.

We need not, however, leap to the conclusion that because corporal punishment was in the past so often used in the wrong way on the wrong persons for the wrong offences, it should automatically be abolished. It ought to be avoided if possible, but there are still times when, in all the circumstances, it is the most effective answer to wrong-doing. The bully and the deliberate trouble-maker can often be more effectively deterred by a prompt and thorough caning than by any other method, and we should not allow the sentimental flinchings of the theorists to prevent us from doing what needs to be done.

CHAPTER EIGHT

A LITTLE LEARNING

Few institutions have been more successful than schools in showing how to hasten slowly. In the days of Aelfric, boy monks were taught Latin under the threat of a flogging; and nearly a thousand years later pupils in a host of English schools could be found learning the same Latin under the same threat, though the threat, from the lips of a Keate or a Butler, had become rather more real.

Let it be admitted that a feverish desire for change is often an unhealthy sign. Still, the unchallenged supremacy of the Classics in so many schools for so long a period does remain a fantastic feature of English education.

Originally, of course, the learning of Latin was sensible and practical. In days when this was the accepted language of the Church and the Law, and when these were the only professions, bar the Army, open to men of ambition, then to learn Latin was simply vocational training, as down to earth as shorthand and typing in a modern commercial school, or engineering in a technical college. In a sense, indeed, the grammar schools of medieval England were the technical schools of their day, teaching the techniques which future churchmen and lawyers would require.

After the Reformation, Latin ceased to have quite the same stranglehold on society. England developed her own language, and its inportance grew steadily. At the beginning of the sixteenth century Sir Thomas More naturally wrote his *Utopia* in Latin. At the beginning of the seventeenth Sir Walter Raleigh as naturally turned to English for his *History of the*

World, and even before this, educationists such as Ascham and Mulcaster had stressed the importance of English.

There was still, however, quite a good case for making Latin the main subject of the school curriculum. It was not yet a dead language. It was still a universal tongue in which philosophers, for instance, could communicate with and to each other, no matter where they were born or in what language they asked their families to pass the salt. Moreover, until the end of the seventeenth century, there was not much else to teach. Scientific knowledge was almost in its infancy, and English literature was mainly contemporary or nearly contemporary.

By the eighteenth century the case for the Classics had grown much weaker. The Royal Society was fully established in 1660 for 'improving Natural Knowledge'; electricity, the telescope, the barometer, and the circulation of the blood, were all known. Spenser, Shakespeare, Marlowe, Jonson, and Raleigh, to name no others, had all been dead long enough to have become established literary figures, and Milton and Dryden were already notable men of letters. There was a body of English literature waiting to be studied.

Yet Latin still remained King of the curriculum, with Greek as queen consort; and the two went on reigning in the public schools, and in many grammar schools too, for nearly another two hundred years.

One cannot but ask why; and there are several possible answers. The first is, of course, the natural conservatism of any person who holds a particular post by virtue of a particular qualification. All existing headmasters were classicists; and to deny the supreme importance of classical studies would have been to cast doubts on their own fitness as instructors. This by itself, however, would not have maintained the overwhelming supremacy of the Classics if it had not been that a certain knowledge, however mild, of Latin and Greek helped to indicate class superiority in days when class distinctions were very real. It would be shallow to grow indignant over

A London Dame School in 1870

this snob value of the Classics. Every age and every place has its own type of snobbery. In the eighteenth and nineteenth centuries the upper section of the middle classes looked upon some acquaintance with the dead languages as a sort of caste mark, and those who felt themselves to belong to this caste were quite prepared to accept that their schools should devote great attention to teaching the distinguishing symbol. Many scholars, moreover, really believed that the study of the Classics did help to train the mind and character.

But perhaps the most formidable buttress to the Classics was the sheer indifference of most upper and middle class parents to what went on in the schools to which they packed off their children. Let Squire Brown—a fictitious character but one as true to life as Polonius—speak for them as Tom awaits the Rugby stage-coach:

'I don't care a straw for Greek particles or the digamma; no more does his mother . . . If he'll only turn out a brave, helpful, truth-telling Englishman, and a gentleman, and a Christian, that's all I want.' It was no unworthy desire, though one cannot help feeling that he might well have tackled the job himself. But it helps to make clear why it was that masters at public schools and private schools were for so long able to give their pupils so restricted an intellectual diet.

One must avoid exaggeration. The dominance of the Classics was confined to certain types of school. At village schools and charity schools the three R's for boys and the two N's (Needlework and Knitting) for girls formed the bulk of the curriculum. An enthusiastic teacher might well add Geography and History, but Latin was a subject out of this world, as Thomas Cooper (himself a working-class boy who had made good) found in the eighteen-thirties when he tried to teach it to the sons of working-class parents.

'We want our Jack to larn to write a good hand,' they complained. 'What's the use of his larnin' Latin? It will nivver be no use to him.'

Nor did every private school intended for the children of

wealthier parents pay deep homage to Caesar and Cicero. At the Bristol school attended by Southey in 1782, where the pupils came mostly from the fairly well-off middle classes, the lessons were mainly in writing and arithmetic, with only a little French, and even less Latin.

Conversely, many public schools did make some attempt to range beyond the walls of Rome, even though they did not venture far. French was sometimes taught; though, one suspects, rather to provide the pupils with a master to make a butt of than to enable them to learn a foreign language. Official evidence on this matter is not always reliable. The French Master at Winchester, in evidence before the Public Schools Commission in 1863, stated that he was well satisfied with the progress made in French. 'The poor man must have been easily satisfied,' A. F. Leach, one of his ex-pupils, commented.

A little Maths was not uncommon. At Harrow it was taught by that much ragged Frenchman, M. Marillier, who taught his pupils to call the subject 'Teek' from his pronunciation of 'Les Mathématiques.' At any rate they learnt this amount of French: it seems that they learnt little else from him during his half-century at the school.

At Winchester the level of teaching appears to have been fairly similar. 'I went to the school [in 1840],' says the Rev. W. Tuckwell, 'at twelve years old able to work a quadratic equation well, and left it at eighteen, competent to perform the same task badly, and my experience was that of most other boys.' Here, and at most other public schools, subjects such as French and Maths either did not count at all in the term's marks or counted so little as to be of no significance.

English was usually taken for granted—not altogether wisely. Cotton Minchin records that he was told by Dr Butler of a boy in the Upper Sixth at Harrow, one of the swells of the school, who thought that Shakespeare and Sir Walter Scott were contemporaries who lived in the reign of Queen Anne. A pupil at Winchester in the eighteen-forties wrote only two English compositions in six years, one of them being a translation from the *Aeneid*. Fifty years later neglect of English in most public schools was still absolute. 'We did no English at Westminster,' said A. A. Milne. 'In my seven years there we never wrote so much as one essay for Authority.'

Sometimes the master excused the slenderness of his curriculum by arguments which to him were no doubt perfectly sound, as did Dr James, a notable eighteenth-century headmaster of Rugby. 'Young people,' he maintained, 'are narrow-necked vessels into which you cannot pour much at a time without waste and running over.' Sometimes he did not bother to offer any excuses at all, as in the case of Dr Sleath, High Master of St Paul's in the early nineteenth century. 'At St Paul's we teach nothing but Classics. If you want your son to learn anything else you must have him taught at home.'

With or without excuses, the flood of Latin and Greek swept over English schools. At Shrewsbury School, in Elizabethan times, the pupil was expected to know some Latin before he was accepted, in addition to being able to write his own name. Other schools were less fussy. At Harrow, for example, they were prepared not only to introduce the young pupil to Latin, but also to teach him to write. At Eton in the eighteenth century nothing at all was taught in the first form except Latin grammar. The second form read the Testament in Latin and the fables of Phaedrus; and the list of authors to be studied grew steadily as the pupil advanced, till the intellectual giants of the sixth had to translate Homer not into their vulgar mother tongue but into Latin. Charles Wordsworth's Greek Grammar, used at Winchester, was also written in Latin, to make obscurity more obscure. 'It remains to me to this day,' said Leach, 'the ideal of all that is hateful and hideous in learning.'

In a regular week at Eton the Fifth and Sixth—who together constituted the Master's division and numbered about 120 boys—had to attend classes seventeen times, ten for construing

The Latin Lesson, 1761

and seven for repetition. The great school for repetition, however, was Winchester. This school had a ceremony known as 'Standing Up' which took place towards the end of one term. Every boy below the two top forms had to learn and recite as many lines of Latin or Greek as he could remember—it did not matter what. Marks were awarded, and remarkable feats of memory were achieved. One boy, it is recorded, recited the whole of a Sophocles play without a single mistake, and there were instances of boys reciting 10,000, 13,000 and even 16,000 lines. It took eight lessons to accomplish the last feat, at the rate of 2,000 lines a lesson. In most cases the lines learnt were forgotten within a month, and in all cases the exercise was almost entirely useless. It was abandoned in the 'sixties.

Even more useless was the common practice of making pupils write Latin verses. At least fifteen hours a week were devoted at Winchester to Latin composition. 'On Tuesdays we composed a "verse task," on Thursdays a "prose task," and on Saturdays a "metre task," besides frequent vulguses.' The Vulgus was a Latin epigram of four to six lines which had to be written on some set subject—an exercise which took place usually three or four times a week.

To write verses in any language is an art by itself, and an art in which only the gifted few possess any talent. To write them in Latin, a language in which the length of vowels and syllables plays an important part in conforming to the arbitrary rules of metre, is an art, or knack, quite by itself. Yet every pupil was expected to accomplish this specialised, difficult, and quite profitless task as a matter of course, and was punished if he failed. A good deal of the systematic flogging of this period was performed in the attempt to make pupils achieve an impossible exactness.

'No man,' wrote Steele, 'who has gone through what they call a great school ... but must have seen an ingenuous creature expiring with shame, with pale looks, beseeching sorrow, and silent tears, throw up its honest eyes, and kneel on its tender knees to an inexorable blockhead, to be forgiven a false quantity of a word in making a Latin verse.'

What was most astonishing was the persistence of this peculiar practice. In many public schools it lasted up to the present century, in spite of the criticisms which the obvious absurdities of the system from time to time brought forth.

In 1809 Sydney Smith, doubtless turning an inward eye towards Winchester, pungently condemned it in the pages of the *Edinburgh Review*.

'There are few boys who remain to the age of eighteen or nineteen at a public school without making above ten thousand Latin verses—a greater number than is contained in the *Aeneid*; and after he has made this quantity of verses in a dead language he never makes another as long as he lives . . . In classical learning it seems to be sufficient if the least possible good is gained by the greatest possible exertion.'

Charles Darwin, at Shrewsbury in the 1820's, subsequently looked back in anger at his wasted years of youth.

'Nothing could have been worse for my mind than this school, as it was strictly classical, nothing else being taught, except a little ancient geography and history . . . Especial attention was paid to verse making, and this I could never do well. I had many friends and got together a good collection of old verses, which, by patching together, sometimes aided by other boys, I could work into any subject.'

Fifty years later the same old grind was being pursued at Eton by a slightly different technique.

'Several hours each week,' says Viscount Cecil of Chelwood (Lord Robert Cecil), 'were consumed in trying to string together Latin verses . . . It consisted in taking a rough Latin version of the sense required and then banging it about with the help of dictionaries and a volume called a Gradus until it was beaten into the spondees and dactyls necessary to constitute the required hexameters and pentameters. A strangely futile occupation.'

The story was still similar in the 'nineties, as Sir Patrick Hastings, an old Carthusian, reported. 'Personally,' he added, 'I could never understand why a small boy was expected to write verses in Greek, at a time when he could scarcely write his own name in English.'

One of the strangest things about the monopoly of attention which the Classics secured for so long was that in spite of it all, only a few boys became even moderately competent Latinists. English teachers today are sometimes blamed by the ignorant or unthinking for failing to turn every pupil into a well-read man or woman with a fluent prose style and a B.B.C. accent. To achieve this impossible task they are lucky if they can snatch five short periods a week. Yet the Latinist who devoted twenty hours of school time, to say nothing of his so-called leisure, to his solitary subject, often remained, after all his devotions, a classical ignoramus.

The method of teaching was sometimes, especially in the lower forms, magnificently negative.

'The day after my entry into this colossal institution [Christ's Hospital] a Latin Grammar was placed in my hands. It was a bulky book of its kind . . . Over a space of years we went systematically through that book; page after page, chapter after chapter. It was all unintelligible, all obscure.' This particular victim was D'Arcy Thompson, an intelligent pupil who subsequently became an intelligent schoolmaster.

The Report of the Royal Commission on the Public Schools in 1864 showed that other schools were achieving a similarly negative result in many directions.

'If a youth after four or five years spent at school, quits it at nineteen, unable to construe an easy bit of Latin or Greek without the help of a dictionary, or to write Latin grammatically, almost ignorant of geography and of the history of his own country, unacquainted with any modern language but his own, and hardly competent to write English correctly . . . his intellectual education must certainly be accounted a failure.'

The Report did not suggest that this result was quite typical, but it was far more common, they declared, than it ought to be.

Twenty years later there is a familiar ring to the experiences of Viscount Cecil at prep school and at Eton.

'When I went up to the University after twelve or fourteen years' tuition in the classical languages I was unable to read even the easiest Latin authors for pleasure.' And he adds: 'We were taught no English literature . . . nor do I remember learning any history.'

Deficiencies in the classical knowledge of young pupils were not due, especially in earlier days, to lack of time. Not only was the time-table choked with Latin and Greek. The hours of work would produce an official strike in any modern trade union. A normal hour for starting school work was seven o'clock in the morning. Elizabethan Eton boys rose at 5 a.m. and began work at six o'clock. At Westminster, in the seventeenth century, the boys were called at 5.15 a.m. with the Latin equivalent of 'Wakey-wakey!' After Latin prayers they went into the cloisters to wash under the pump, and began morning school by 6 a.m. at the latest. After two hours of work they were allowed to turn their thoughts from *amo* or the *Aeneid* to breakfast. Harrow pupils were even tougher. They too began work at six o'clock, but their first lesson lasted for five hours, ending at 11 a.m.

It was at Harrow, moreover, in the 1820's, that one of the masters, a poor sleeper, roused his class at 4 a.m. so that he could 'relieve the tedium of the night' with an early-morning lesson.

Private schools were often no softer. Gilbert Wakefield, at a school near Nottingham in 1763, had to be *in the school-room* by 5 a.m. in summer, and stayed there for thirteen hours, till 6 p.m., with less than two hours off for breakfast and dinner. In spite of the master's incredible devotion to duty, Wakefield records that he learnt 'literally nothing.'

On the whole, however, there has been a steady tendency for lesson hours to follow the principle described by the Gryphon to Alice, growing less, if not from day to day, then at least from century to century. The process is clearly seen at Harrow. In the seventeenth century First School was from 6 a.m. till 11 a.m. In the eighteenth it was from 7.30 a.m. till 9 a.m. By the twentieth century the lesson finished at 8.15 a.m., and after the First World War it lasted for only thirty-five minutes and began a quarter of an hour later in winter.

Holidays, on the contrary, have tended to acquire a middle-aged spread. In the sixteenth century Shrewsbury School, for example, had no summer holiday at all. The only respite from school, apart from a week at Whitsun, was a little over a fortnight at Christmas and a little under at Easter. At Eton during the same era there was only one real holiday, a period of three weeks in May; and any boy who tried to steal an extra day was flogged as soon as he returned.

By the beginning of the nineteenth century schools were a little less overwhelming, but the holidays would still not be regarded as generous by modern pupils accustomed to receiving over a quarter of the year to themselves. At Lewisham Congregational School, for instance, the only continuous holiday was a six-weeks' period in July and August. For the remaining ten and a half months the boys remained at the school even when a holiday from work was granted. A day or two after Christmas, a day or two before Easter, and the king's birthday were the only full-day breaks.

Some schools were more generous with holidays from work, especially in the summer. In the eighteen-forties Winchester used commonly to offer two and a half days a week, in addition to Sunday, as a 'Remedy'—which meant that although the boys were supposed to go into school for an hour or two, no master was present to take a lesson, and no work was done. A quaint and rather fatuous tradition was followed. The 'Remedy' was not fixed as a standing order, but had to be requested each time by the head prefect, who was presented by the headmaster with a gold ring for the day if the holiday was granted. (Great was the perturbation one evening when it was discovered that the ring had been lost.) The 'Remedies' were always Tuesday and Thursday, with Friday as a half, which would have made an agreeably short working week if it had not been that for fags, at any rate, the leisure hours were often far more burdensome than the time spent at lessons.

Although holidays tended to expand as the years went by, some schools were remarkably grudging over breaks during the day. The church school in Whitechapel that George Lansbury attended in the eighteen-seventies had no playtime at all. The future Labour leader got up an agitation to have this grievance removed, pointing out that the parents paid four-pence a week, whereas the charity school kids in an adjacent building paid nothing at all for their education and yet had the benefit of the large playground between the schools. His plea was successful.

The schoolroom in which a pupil's long and often laborious hours were spent was often singularly lacking in simple amenities, especially warmth. Well into the nineteenth century we find strange conditions recorded.

At Harrow, during that tedious first lesson, a solitary faggot blazed for a short while in the large schoolroom; it was never replenished. Still, this was better than at Blundell's, where sleet used to drift through the roof and drip upon the boys' copy-books, or the Congregational School, Lewisham, where the schoolroom (the headmaster complained) 'was completely flooded during the recent rains, and it is impossible to say how long the boys may retain their health while obliged to sit for days half shoe-deep in water.' This schoolroom had originally been designed for, and used as, a stable, so we are not surprised to learn—as the headmaster mildly says in a report—that 'consequently it was never well adapted to its present purpose.'

At Marlborough, as at a good many other schools, there was

for many years only one room for the three hundred boys to spend their waking hours in; and this room, in which they had to work during lesson times and play during their leisure, was 'warmed' by a couple of open fires. In the depths of a Wiltshire winter the smaller boys would never see the flames except from their remote desks, and the only time they felt any warmth (as one old Marlburian remarked bitterly) was when they were tortured by 'roasting.'

The boys at Hastings Grammar School suffered from an opposite ordeal. 'My classroom chimney does not merely smoke,' the headmaster reported to the governors: 'the flames leap out at right angles into the room, filling it with blacks. The boys sit in a bitterly cold draught in the midst of dense smoke.'

At schools situated in large cities the main problem was that masters were so often liable to be seen and not heard. We tend to think of our own period as an Age of Noise, as indeed it is, but we must not forget that even jet planes and motor-cycles, though their din is far-reaching, cannot beat, for immediate disturbance, the clatter of innumerable horses' hooves on a cobbled street just outside a school window. At St Paul's in the 'sixties the staff could easily have been driven to Bedlam if they had allowed the conditions of work to worry them. 'The boys can talk *aloud* to one another with perfect impunity,' said the senior master, 'and are almost compelled to do so if any communication at all is to be allowed to them; while the Masters necessarily occasion serious interruption to each other in the attempt to make themselves heard.'

The inconvenience of holding several classes in a single room became so obvious, especially as new subjects were added to the curriculum, that by the end of the nineteenth century the practice had almost disappeared. But some very odd classrooms often resulted, such as the 'Dog Kennel' at Eton in the 'sixties—a room about fifteen feet square, with a few low benches on one side and a stool and master's desk on the other.

A pupil in a back bench who required to leave his place could only do so by climbing over the shoulders of the boys in front. If written exercises were set, the boys had to write on their knees unless another room could be found. In this they were following Elizabethan precedent. 'When they have to write, let them use their knees for a table,' ordered one of the Statutes of Bury Grammar School.

Harrow had its 'turret room,' lit by little slits of windows and reached by a narrow winding staircase. There was no heating except by tiny gas jets, intended, rather hopefully, to give illumination. On a cold winter's morning before breakfast the seventy-five minutes' lesson could proceed as slowly as a frost-bitten sledge-puller in the Antarctic. Another classroom here was an old attic in the headmaster's house. The master's desk was in the middle of the room, while the boys sat with their backs to him, facing sloping boards which served as desks. This peculiar arrangement somewhat nullified the value of the blackboard and easel thoughtfully placed at the master's elbow.

It would, of course, be wrong to suggest that the public and grammar schools had a monopoly of bad conditions. Some of the old Dame Schools were particularly notorious. An inspector of the 1840's found, especially in manufacturing districts, many so-called schools kept by elderly widows in messy living-rooms which stank horribly, where half the children 'were without any means whatever in employing their time.' Even in the better village schools it was common to find not a single window open. As late as 1900 writing-books were scarce in some areas. 'I do not remember using an exercise book except at an examination,' said George Tomlinson, Labour Minister of Education after the Second World War. 'Slates were always used instead.' Classes were often very large. My mother, who taught in London Board Schools of this period, had eighty or ninety pupils in her class, including a dozen mentally deficient children.

It needs only to be added that good work was often done

by good teachers in the worst possible conditions in these primitive times, just as poor work can easily be done in the centrally-heated classroom of a modern comprehensive school equipped with radiogram, television, and electrically-operated window-blinds.

CHAPTER NINE

CREATURES GREAT AND SMALL

CONTRARY to popular opinion, prefects were not invented by Dr Arnold. In some form or another they have existed as long as schools.

William of Wykeham made special provision for them when he founded Winchester College. 'In each of the lower chambers let there be at least three scholars of good repute, more advanced than the others in age, sense, and learning, to superintend the studies of their chamber-fellows, and diligently oversee them.' Even Wykeham was not thinking up something novel. A similar provision is found in the Statutes of Merton College, Oxford, 1274, undergraduates in these early days often being much younger than they are today.

Eton naturally followed Winchester's lead. 'Two prepositors in every form, which doth give in a scroll the absent names at any lecture. Also two prepositors in the body of the church . . . Prepositors in the field when they play, for fighting, rent clothes, black eyes, or such like. Prepositors for ill-kept heads, unwashed faces, foul clothes, and such other . . .'

These early prefects differed from their late counterparts in having no power of punishment. They were informers, not governors. Their task was to accuse offenders. 'By their example and warning,' says Robert Matthew (in Latin verse) in the seventeenth century, 'they keep the rule of the school, and if any madcaps and rowdy ones rebel, their names are put on a roll, and the roll is given to the master, who sets all right with the four-forked rod.'

'Power tends to corrupt,' was the famous opinion of Lord Acton; and the power possessed by the official informer lends itself peculiarly to corruption, as modern police-states have shown. In 1668 the complaint was made at Winchester: 'That the Inferiors are many times forced to make the beds of Prefects, and likewise to supply them with ink, paper, and such-like implements, or else they are forced to run the hazard of being accused.' Thus the prefect system was already leading to the fagging system.

As Masters tended to leave their pupils more and more to their own devices (contrary to founders' wishes), prefects developed greater powers, and fags became semi-official slaves. Masters, Wardens, and Provosts grew conveniently short-sighted and hard of hearing when lessons were over, assuring themselves, from time to time, that it was a good thing for boys to learn to govern themselves. The absolute powers that prefects tended to assume out of school were either officially recognised or tacitly accepted.

By the end of the eighteenth century the prefect system was in full swing at almost all of the public schools except Eton, where the senior boys used the privileges of prefectship without assuming the title. Prefects were now becoming more than mere accusers: they were law-makers, policemen, magistrates, and executioners combined.

The power to inflict corporal punishment became one of their most jealously-guarded privileges, and one of their most frequently used rights. No doubt at times the infliction was just and timely. The worthy Holmes, we recall, administered a good sound thrashing to a bully, and was in later years sought out and thanked. But even apart from the fact that *Tom Brown's Schooldays* is a work of fiction, this was in the days of Arnold, when praepostors were very much the Doctor's trusted help-meets. In less enlightened conditions the justice of a prefect's flogging was often less evident.

A common practice at the pre-Arnoldian Rugby was for these all-powerful young men to send their victims to a copse two miles distant (and out of bounds) to gather stout ash-saplings with which to be chastised. No mercy was shown.

One boy, it is recorded in the 1790's, was compelled to go to the copse three times in the course of a single thrashing, two of these strong sticks being broken over his body before the prefect tired of the punishment.

The prefects were often not merely tyrants but also cowardly tyrants, with no sense of honest dealing. Early in the nineteenth century, for example, a Rugby boy of thirteen was sent, in the usual way, to Grime's Spinney to steal ash-plants to be beaten with. He was caught on the way by the headmaster, Dr Ingles, who demanded the name of the prefect. The boy, following the schoolboys' queer code of honour (or perhaps afraid to speak out), would not give the required name. The headmaster boxed his ears, and ultimately expelled him. Yet the prefect concerned had no thought of coming forward to exonerate the victim of his own action, nor did it occur to the other prefects that there was any moral compulsion for him to do so. Least of all, apparently, did it strike the headmaster that it was his duty to put pressure on his prefects to act like honest men.

Even in Arnold's time, and for some years afterwards, the Sixth were allowed a freedom to knock their juniors about that seems to us excessive. As many as *sixty* strokes with the ash-plant were permitted. When the number was reduced to twelve in 1854, the prefects were quite indignant at being robbed of a cherished heritage.

The capricious tyranny of the Christ's Hospital prefects has been made unforgettable by Charles Lamb, as well as many another Old Blue.

'The oppressions of these young brutes are heart-sickening to call to recollection. I have been called out of my bed, and *waked for the purpose*, in the coldest winter nights—and this not once but night after night—in my shirt, to receive the discipline of the leather thong, with eleven other sufferers, because it pleased my callow overseer, when there has been any talking heard after we were gone to bed, to make the last six beds in the dormitory, where the youngest children of us slept [two in a bed], answerable for an offence they neither dared to commit nor had the power to hinder.'

Reform was slow in coming.

'I have had some experience of pretty sharp discipline in my time,' wrote an Old Blue of a period thirty years later than Elia's, 'but the remembrance of past canings and floggings is nothing to me now in comparison with the bitter recollection of the treatment received at the hands of some of the monitors.' If one of them took a dislike to a boy he was able not only to persecute the youngster himself but, by false accusations and other ways, to put him on bad terms with other boys and even the Master and the Steward. 'The monitors were accustomed, according to my experience, to use their fists very freely, and I never knew one of them called to account for the practice.'

'To find a kind monitor was the exception,' another old boy of the school commented, and A. J. Butler, speaking of the late eighteen-sixties, added: 'The monitors were often excessively tyrannical. There was very little to control their temper or power.'

A semi-official history of Charterhouse records that at the old London school the monitors had unlimited powers, and often made the fags' lives a burden to them. The masters almost never interfered.

But the two schools, above all others, where prefectorial privilege was dominant were Winchester and Harrow.

By the beginning of the nineteenth century the 'scholars of good repute' desired as overseers by William of Wykeham had become hefty young athletes determined to enforce their own wishes on their juniors, and able to persuade their Master to accept the position as inevitable. Dr Goddard, Master of Winchester from 1793 till 1809, endeavoured to make the best of what was really a *fait accompli* by the older boys, trying to show trust in them to exercise a judicious self-government. He had at least success enough to inspire his most serious-minded Sixth Former to achieve a much greater success at ` ugby; but the fact that one of the trusted Winchester prefects could brag of threatening to stab an innocent woman shows that authority and barbarity could go very well together.

The unchecked brutality of Winchester prefects has been revealed by many different observers, and cannot be laughed off. Young Walter Hook was not being wildly melodramatic when he wrote to his brother (happily absent from school):

'I hate this place more and more every day. I was licked yesterday [by prefects] more severely than ever before. I cannot run or holloa out loud even now without hurting my side, and am to be licked again today for cutting football to write this. Yet I should not be able to write at another time as I go at top of hall [*i.e.*, on tap for unlimited fagging] and get so much to do. I begin to fear my licking. If I am killed, as I think I shall be, tell the school butler to send you my books.'

This letter was considered 'irresistibly droll' by Hook's biographer. His sense of humour was enviable. True, Hook did not die from his severe licking, but lived to become a sturdy boy strong enough to knock down a bully who sneered at Shakespeare, and later still, pious enough to become Dean of Chichester. But his fears at the age of fourteen were not so funny as they may seem to readers and writers of comfortable middle-age in a later era. The Rev. W. Tuckwell, at Winchester in the eighteen-forties, speaks of a common tradition, rife in his day, of a tremendous thrashing which a prefect had formerly delivered to a victim who had barely escaped with his life. And if this seems like a yarn (spun by the Fat Boy of Wykeham) intended to scare greenhorns, let Mr Tuckwell speak from his own personal knowledge.

'The worst tunding I ever saw was inflicted by a college prefect on a commoner, and though nominally official, was accentuated by personal resentment. The boy made no cry, but reckoned audibly the 150 cuts as they fell; then was for some days in danger.' The prefect in this instance was reprimanded by being deprived of his office; but this mild penalty was inflicted only because the victim's father was a man of sufficient consequence to make a fuss.

'I remember many other cases,' Tuckwell adds, 'in which the right of tunding [*i.e.* thrashing with a heavy stick] was atrociously abused.'

One such case has been recorded by another Wykehamist, also (in most matters) an admirer of his old school.

'My old friend Dummy . . . was handed over to a tutor (prefect) who, by way of taking a great interest in his pupil, prevented other boys from thrashing him by operating on him so constantly himself that they scarcely had any chance of so doing. The tutor, tall, thin, bullet-headed . . . used from time to time to conduct his pupil into a quiet corner, and, with a cheerful smile beaming on his countenance, would give himself a few minutes healthy, but not too violent, exercise . . . He was not very muscular, or the consequences might have been serious. As it was, whenever Dummy went to bathe, a number of spectators always assembled to see his back, which, from the nape of his neck to his ankles, was a network of intersecting bruises.'

Anthony Trollope was at Winchester, where he came under the tutorship of his elder brother, Thomas Adolphus. In later life the two were good friends; yet such was the influence of Winchester upon a fundamentally decent boy that the elder brother, 'as part of his daily exercise,' thrashed his pupil regularly with a heavy stick. 'That such thrashings should have been possible at a school as a continual part of one's daily life,' the novelist comments, mildly enough, 'seems to me to argue a very ill condition of school discipline.'

From time to time glimpses of the obvious reached the eyes of authority, and even penetrated to the more humane and sensible prefects. The degrading of a ferocious prefect has already been mentioned. When Tuckwell was at the top of the school, he himself took a share in bringing about a similar demotion. A case of cruel bullying by a college prefect came to his notice. 'I took counsel with the other seniors, and in our joint names cautioned him. On his persisting I brought the offence before the Warden.' This is certainly a big step forward from the dog-does-not-eat-dog attitude adopted by most seniors at the big schools. But even here, the only punishment suffered by the bully was loss of office; and it is clear that bullying by a prefect had to be violent and persistent in the face of warning in order to be dealt with at all. Moreover, no precautions seem to have been taken to see that the bullying did not continue on the sly: the bully remained untouched, and on the premises.

After a hundred years of barely-checked freedom, the Divine Right of Winchester prefects to 'tund' a chosen victim gradually ceased to operate. Its collapse was hastened by an affair which became known as the Great Tunding Row. Oddly enough the cause of the row, though serious, was far less flagrant than any of the previous cases I have cited; but consciences were no doubt developing softer spots.

In October 1872 the prefects decided to tighten up the discipline in a certain house by holding an examination in the conventions and slang words of the school, commonly known as 'Notions.' A seventeen-year-old senior boy naturally objected to being subjected to a test which was ordinarily given only to new-boy fags. He refused to attend the examination, and when the prefects wished to punish him he appealed to the headmaster, Dr Ridding. The case was too clear even for a headmaster to evade the issue entirely. The prefects were obviously in the wrong in treating a senior boy as a junior, and the boy was fully justified in objecting. Dr Ridding accepted this and supported the appeal, but at the same time, in true headmasterly fashion, he also supported the opposite view, that the boy, as a matter of discipline, should really have done as the prefects told him.

The prefects had no intention of facing both ways at once. They ignored that part of the headmaster's judgement which supported the appeal, called the boy to a special meeting, and proceeded to deliver a drastic tunding of thirty-one blows.

The boy's father came to hear of the affair, and was naturally angry. It found its way into the newspapers, notably *The*

Times; and the Governing Body of the college inquired into the whole matter of prefectorial punishments. They condemned the prefects' action, expressed disapproval of corporal punishment by prefects for minor offences, and hoped that the absurd examination in 'Notions' would disappear. They also endeavoured to set all right with the outside world by having 'learnt with satisfaction' that the headmaster had already tidied up the garden and that their suggestions had already been anticipated.

They were, of course, being unduly optimistic: reforms are not so easily carried out. W. H. David, who was head prefect a few years later, states explicitly that 'even when our community was shaken by what was known as the "Tunding Row," and much that had been hidden was brought to light, things did not change for the better at once.' He also gives the lie to those over-patriotic Old Boys who pretended (or possibly believed) that there had never been any weeds in the garden. 'I saw enough cruelty and misery in my first weeks [before the row] to gather that the evil was coming to a head,' and he makes it clear that the notoriety which Winchester brought upon herself was both deserved and salutary.

A somewhat similar disturbance had occurred at Harrow nearly twenty years earlier, when the repercussions were even more far-reaching. Two noble families were set at loggerheads, the headmaster was brought into controversial relationship with the Home Secretary, while *The Times* came out with a long and pontifical leading article and had its correspondence columns almost monopolised by monitorial opponents and supporters. And all because of a remark made by one boy to another during a game!

In the course of a game of football one day in April 1854 a boy named Stewart, the son of the Earl of Galloway, addressed some offensive remark (which was never made public) to another boy. A monitor, the son of Baron Platt, spoke sharply to Stewart, who retorted equally sharply. Next morning Platt sent for Stewart and ordered him to submit to a thrashing.

Stewart objected, and finally appealed to the headmaster, Dr Vaughan. He was advised to submit to the prefect's decision, and did so; whereupon Platt, in the presence of the other monitors, gave him thirty-one strokes (again the magic number) with a cane. The flogging was, in fact, so severe that the victim had to receive medical attention.

Strangely enough, it was not Stewart or his father who began the public row. Dr Vaughan was so annoyed at the excessive punishment that he degraded Platt, to the extreme and open indignation of his father the Baron. Lord Galloway now joined in, demanding redress for *his* son; and the two distinguished families publicly let fly at each other. Harrow was now very much in the news.

The manager of *The Times*, John Walter III, had been educated at Eton, which prided itself on its individualistic freedom from the monitorial system. This plain example of monitorial misconduct, above all at Harrow (already Eton's rival), provided an opportunity too good to miss.

'We must now pronounce [said a leading article], without a moment's hesitation, that the monitorial system, as illustrated in the case before us, is entirely indefensible . . . The whole transaction took place out of school, and in the middle of a game of football. The remarks on both sides had exclusive reference to the game, and were called forth by the incidents . . . In one half of his character Platt was a schoolboy, playing with his fellows, and open to all the give and take that a boy's game occasions. In the other half of his character he was sacred, and entitled to all kinds of deferential regard.' The moral, *The Times* insisted, was that 'every boy at school is entitled to receive such supervision as he requires, at the hands of the proper masters,' and that prefects should not be allowed to supervise other boys, still less administer corporal punishment.

Many old public school men came to the support of the monitorial system, especially from Rugby. But there could be no real defence either of Platt's exaggerated sense of prefectorial dignity or of the headmaster's handling of the difficulty.

His excessive eagerness for the prefects to run the school in their own way left an open path to wrong action. The proper redress for a hasty word at football was an apology to the prefect concerned, and then both justice and the dignity of office would have been left intact. Had Vaughan offered this advice to both sides instead of advising a meek submission to the callow judgment and rough habits of his prefects he might have saved himself and his school from a good deal of worry and the monitorial system from a great deal of abuse.

We must not, however, ignore the difficulties that faced these nineteenth-century headmasters. Some form of monitorial system existed in almost every boarding-school, whether it was known under that name or not. The senior boys always exercised power over their juniors, either officially or otherwise; and now headmasters, especially since Arnold had shown the way, were trying to get the prefects to exploit this power for the benefit of the school. Whether it was well done or badly done depended to a large extent on the personality of the headmaster. Mistakes in harnessing this potent Sixth Form influence were in any case inevitable.

At one school in particular the prefect system had justified itself beyond all dispute. When Mr Cotton came to Marlborough in 1851 he found monitors who had most of the privileges of rank without the responsibilities. Boys below the Fourth Form had to remove their caps to these great men, whose duties, however, were largely limited to calling out names and reporting offenders. They had no hand in governing the school, except to lead it, on occasion, to sudden mutiny.

Mr Cotton was determined that his prefects must play a leading part in putting down abuses, especially (to start with) in matters such as the breaking of bounds and pub-crawling. He was able to inspire them to devote half-holidays to searching the public-houses within a radius of four miles from the school, sometimes with startling results.

The other boys at first resented the part played by prefects

in interfering with Marlborough College customs of drunkenness and lawlessness. But Mr Cotton was as explicit with the
boys as he had been with the governors.

'The Council informed me on my appointment,' he told
the assembled school, 'that the College was in a bad state of
discipline, and they hoped I would allow no boys to go out
except walking in lines with a master in charge. I told them
I could not accept office on such terms, that the school I hoped
to govern was a public school not a private one, and I would
try and make it govern itself by means of prefects.

'The School now knows how matters stand. They must
either submit to the prefects or be reduced to the level of a
private school and have their freedom ignominiously curtailed.
The prefects are, and shall be, so long as I am Head, the rulers
of this school. As soon as I see this is impracticable I will
resign.'

There was perhaps a certain snobbery in Mr Cotton's
references to private schools. But Marlborough, in any case,
was too big to function satisfactorily as a private school. If
the prefect system would not work, the chaos which had
brought the College almost to disaster would continue.

The system did work. Not perfectly, for boys are far from
perfect, and there was as yet no tradition of prefectship. But
a sense of order developed, not least because Mr Cotton kept
his finger on the pulse of the system, and did not make the
mistake of allowing rulership by prefects to become abdication
by the headmaster.

When unwisdom by his lieutenants brought the system into
disrepute, he himself was ready to step forward and iron out
the problems. On one occasion three prefects captured a dog
which was being used by a young sportsman on his quite illicit
hunting expeditions. He and his companions were sent back for
future punishment, while the prefects took charge of the dog.
Finding it difficult to make it come with them they hanged it
from a tree. An ugly situation developed in the school when
this brutal action became known, and was only saved by a

speech to the school by the headmaster, in which the prefects' error was frankly admitted and half-humorously excused.

The difficulties attached to the prefect system have never been fully resolved. If the prefects have no right of rulership and no power of punishment to enforce the rules, they tend to lose their influence on the school's conduct or even to become active leaders in the wrong direction. If they are given the power to punish, and especially to employ corporal punishment, they tend to misuse it. There are powerful arguments against older boys being given the right to strike younger boys.

'We believe,' says one modern educationist, 'that the benefits of the prefectorial system are too much taken for granted . . . particularly where boys are appointed prefects solely because of athletic prowess. The handling of small boys demands sympathy and knowledge which it must not be too lightly assumed every athletic youth possesses. It is often forgotten that the prefect system is not self-government. It is the most autocratic form of government.'

Too often the system has been apt to work out very much as Charles Graves found it at Charterhouse just before and during the First World War.

'Any boy who failed to play the requisite number of games was beaten with a toasting-fork, which was rather worse than being beaten with a cane. One was beaten, really, for almost anything. An unfortunate American youth called Dunne was beaten for refusing to cheer on the sideline during one of the house football matches. New boys were beaten if they were unable to pass a local knowledge examination after their first fortnight.'

Some schools have endeavoured to safeguard against abuses of the prefectorial right to beat by allowing an appeal to the headmaster. In practice the right of appeal has usually turned out to be nominal and worthless.

'Any boy condemned to any punishment by a Master or prefect had a right of appeal to the headmaster, and was told,

The Fag (by Lewis Baumer) from *The Lighter Side of School Life*

so,' says F. G. Newbolt, of Clifton College. He adds: 'Appeals were very rare, and I never knew of one being successful.'

The exact way in which the thing works has been penetratingly portrayed by A. A. Milne. A wretched junior has been summoned before the College Captain and three other monitors sitting in council for the administration of 'justice.'

Captain: You were ragging up-Fields today.

Junior (swallowing): No, I wasn't.

Captain (negligently): Have you any other excuse to make?

Junior (at a loss): No.

Captain (formally and without interest): Do you wish to appeal to the Headmaster?

Junior (wishing to): No.'

The cane is handed to a monitor and the junior bends over and receives four strokes for a casual offence which he possibly has or possibly has not committed. Milne was writing of Westminster in the 'nineties, but the scene is true of almost any public or grammar school where prefects have the right to cane.

Usually no drastic harm is done by what in effect is a subtle form of legal bullying. But no good is done either; and corporal punishment is quite unjustified unless, by taming deliberate insolence or plain bullying, it offers a definite contribution to the well-being of the school state. With very rare exceptions, boys in their 'teens (irresponsible undergraduates at heart) are unsuitable persons to be entrusted with a form of punishment that is always undesirable except as a last resort.

From prefects to fags is a very short step. Many public school men would consider the two to be as inseparable as husband and wife or as toast and marmalade.

In fact, however, there is a significant difference. In the course of time the prefect system has extended, with claws well cut, from the public school to every type of school, including the primary school. Fagging, on the other hand, has tended to decrease greatly in public schools, and does not exist at all in other schools.

The reason is clear enough. Prefects, judiciously appointed and sensibly employed, have a definite and useful part to play in any educational system, valuable to themselves and helpful towards school discipline. Fagging, on the other hand, is simply a survival of the Might-equals-Right attitude. In modern times the spirit has been wonderfully tamed, but it derives from the law of the jungle.

It has already been shown in this chapter that by the sixteenth century, at any rate, lower boys were being forced by monitors to perform menial tasks for them under the threat of being officially accused of some offence. By the eighteenth century the system of fagging was in full swing, though the fag-masters were by no means always prefects. In 1780, we are told, a fag at Rugby would sometimes be made to warm two or three older boys' beds in succession by lying in them; or he might have to rise at an unearthly hour in the morning, run a couple of miles into the country, and take up a night-line which his fag-master had set the previous evening.

By the early nineteenth century fagging had developed into an almost full-time slavery. Here is the time-table of a young boy at Westminster in the year 1807.

6 a.m. Rise, dress, brush fag-master's clothes, clean several of his shoes, go to pump in Dean's Yard for hard water for his teeth, to the cistern at Mother Grant's (boarding-house) for soft water for his hands and face, pass the rest of the time till 8 in washing self or learning morning school lesson.

8–9. In school.

9–10. Get master's breakfast—own breakfast if time.

10–12 a.m. In school.

12–1. In Usher's correcting room preparing for afternoon lessons.

1–2. Dinner in hall. Roll-call. (Food very bad.)

2–5. Evening school.

5–6. Buying bread, butter, milk, eggs, or other food for fag-master's tea, and preparing that meal.

6 next morning. Locked up at Mother Grant's. Engaged till bedtime in miscellaneous fagging.

A young child, not yet nine years old who had endured this continuous drudgery for a fortnight at length gave up in despair. Instead of preparing tea for his lord and master he hid in the coal cellar. Two hours later he was discovered, and handed over to the great man.

'He made me stand at attention, with my little fingers on the seam of my trousers, like a soldier at drill. He then felled me to the ground by a swinging "buckhorse" (a blow with the open hand) on my right cheek. I rose up stupefied and made to resume my former position, and received a second floorer. I know not how often I underwent this ordeal, but I remember going to bed with a racking headache, and being unable to put in an appearance next morning at school.'

Dacres Adams, who was a son of William Pitt's secretary, has left us a vivid account of his life as a junior in the same school in 1820. He had to carry his fag-master's books into school at eight o'clock, remain in school till nine, go into a special room to make birch-rods for half an hour, and then at length have his breakfast. For the next two hours he was in school, for half the time standing near the master's desk, and for the rest of the time being liable to be sent on messages by his seniors. There was an hour's playtime at twelve, but again he was at the beck and call of any senior who might choose to send him on a message. 'At one I go to dinner, where I have to mash some potatoes for my master and brown them before the fire, and to toast his meat. After I have done that I may sit down to dinner, if there is time, for I have only half an hour to do everything. It takes me only four or five minutes to eat my dinner, but sometimes I have not time for it.'

Every fourth day, in addition to giving the usual full attention to his fag-master, he had also to look after ten Third Year boys—'clean their candlesticks, and get candles for them.

I make their ten beds, which takes a great while, for I must do all my master's things just the same. I have to brush clothes for ten fellows, fill eight pitchers, and clean eight basins, to wash up their (ten) sets of tea things when they have tea or coffee, and do sometimes a few other jobs for them. We have no supper . . . I have to clean all the penates that are used, such as grid-irons, frying-pans, Dutch ovens, and saucepans.'

For the privilege of enabling their sons to devote their days to this type of education, parents were now paying up to £100 a year, even though a King's Scholarship had been obtained. Adams withdrew his two sons from the school after a year of this somewhat expensive slavery. By 1841 the numbers at Westminster had fallen to sixty-seven.

At Eton 'the life of a junior was sometimes very miserable indeed. A good deal of his time out of school passed in the combined occupations of valet, cook, housemaid, and shoe-black to his fag-master . . . He might also have to sit up half the night to arrange and attend upon a late Sixth Form supper (frequently including the concoction of a bowl of punch).' A. D. Coleridge suffered the additional disadvantage of having to fag for a senior who was partial to reptiles. 'If you don't take up that snake at once and carry it out to the field you'll find it in your bed tonight,' he was told; so he gingerly smuggled it out of the school in a red pocket-handkerchief.

At Charterhouse in the mid-nineteenth century the twelve juniors (called *basinites*) each took a week in turn to call and valet the monitors. At seven o'clock they had to be roused, and a quarter of an hour later cans of hot water had to be fetched and towels dried. The monitors were called again. Then, as they dressed, all the juniors had to stand in a line against the wall, trying to learn their morning's lesson, but being constantly interrupted by shouts of 'My shoes,' 'My braces,' or 'My gown.' Several times a basinite would be sent to crane his head out of the window to see the time by the chapel clock. At the last possible moment would come the command, 'Fly, basinites,' whereupon the wretched juniors would have to snatch up their own books and gowns and dash wildly to the chapel to escape an entry in the Black Book for being late.

Breakfast came after the first lesson: that is, breakfast for the senior. The junior had to spend his time preparing his fag-master's meal, though sometimes a kind master would allow his fag to have a hasty snack himself. The most unfortunate junior of all was one appointed as milk-fag. He was 'the common slave of all the Uppers,' and also had to spend his time lifting the heavy saucepan on and off the fire. 'He got many a *boxer* and *swinger* [the terms hardly need explaining] if the milk was spilt or smoked.'

But the school where fagging reached the extremest point was probably Winchester College. 'Slavery,' says an ex-pupil of the 1840 period, 'is the only word which sums up the three years' experience of a college junior. Its details, whether cruel or grotesque, were all so contrived as to stamp upon the young boy's mind his grade of servile inferiority . . . Nothing was more resented by the seniors than the faintest manifestation of independent feeling on the part of any fag.'

'A boy may be "valet" to one prefect,' says another writer, ' "breakfast fag" to another, and liable to be sent on errands or to be made to field at cricket at the bidding of any prefect.'

Each prefect and minor official in Chambers (small dormitories) had a valet, whose duties were to prepare tea or coffee in the evening, fetch water in the morning, and carry washing things and books to school after morning chapel, and back in the evening. The Junior Valet was the busiest person in the College, getting up at 5.30 in the morning when the porter rapped on the door, calling the other boys (and often receiving a missile or blow for doing so), lighting a fire, and cleaning the candlesticks, smothered in the previous night's grease. Then he had to fetch his own fag-master's water, and clean out his basin, besides washing himself at the tap in the open court, thawing it first with a lighted faggot in frosty weather.

Throughout this period he had constantly to go out into the court to listen carefully for the chapel bells, calling out 'First peal,' 'Second peal,' or 'Bells down' in turn, and finally announcing the arrival of the headmaster and the Prefect of Chapel (for taking names of late-comers).

After the morning service there was a preparation period of one hour for the purpose of learning the morning lesson. But the junior was lucky if he could snatch more than a few minutes. Cries of 'Junior' would come from the various prefects, and the fag would have to go and oil a cricket bat, or fetch a fives ball from the porter, or go to the gate and call for a messenger to get some coffee or bread and butter for a prefect whose appetite was too impatient to wait for breakfast. No boys were allowed to leave the school court during this period.

At half-past eight came the official breakfast in the Hall. Here the junior was 'breakfast-fag' to some prefect, whose chunk of butter he had to wash and whose sausages or chops he had to fry. In addition to this, he was a table-fag to a group of eight or nine other boys, whose food he had to fetch at the hatches, where there was always a fearful scrimmage. Tea was obtained in mugs from a special table. Knives and forks had to be obtained from one of the hatches, and as there were usually insufficient to go round, some unlucky juniors were unpleasantly rewarded for their failure to find the un-discoverable. The juniors themselves commonly went without knives, 'digging into the butter with a sharp edge of a crust, and eating it in fragmentary lumps alternate with the bread.'

Breakfast was over by 9.30 a.m., and from then until twelve o'clock the junior was in school, 'a comparatively peaceful time.' The hour from noon till one was sacred to games—which meant that the junior spent the time fielding for the seniors' batting practice or acting as a fence at football, as a later chapter will show. Dinner was taken in hall again. The older boys automatically had the saddles, shoulders, and legs of mutton; the juniors had the 'racks,'—long bones with small pieces of meat attached through which the spit had passed, leaving a large green scar.

At the end of the hall was a large chest known as 'Tub,' into which all the food which had not been eaten was thrown, afterwards being distributed to the local poor. One Old Wyke-hamist has recorded that of all the many miseries he endured as a junior, the very worst was to see good meat from the prefects' tables being flung into 'Tub' when he himself, owing to the desperate scramble to wait on his seniors, had had no dinner at all.

Afternoon school lasted for four hours, the boys crowded together in movable desks in the huge schoolroom, lit only by candles. Two prefects armed with the usual ground ash sticks preserved order, lashing out at any boys who they thought were making unnecessary noise,—thus, as their stout sticks often struck desks as well as shoulders, creating more disturbance than the disturbers.

At six o'clock a prefect read a Latin prayer of thanks for the religion and good learning which the Founder's bounty had enabled the pupils to enjoy during the day, and 'the junior relapsed once more into a bondslave: unbroken were his toils during the next hour and a half.' First he had to hurry to Chambers, light the fire, fill the kettle and hang it above the fire, and also fill boilers and coffee-pots and place them on an iron bar in front of the fire. Then he had to rush up to the dining-hall, encountering on the staircase a prefect armed in the usual way, whose rather pointless duty was to hit out at any fag who seemed to be late in coming to the hall. For an hour and a half the fag was once more engaged in his double capacity of slave to his particular fag-master and servant to a particular table. The boys at the latter had to have their beer fetched (it being unthinkable that a boy above the rank of junior should perform any simple service for himself) and their mustard prepared. These minor duties being carried out, the fag got down to the main task of preparing supper for his lord. Potatoes might have to be mashed and fried, meat fried with onions, or cheese toasted—all these operations being performed at a fire which did not allow too many cooks at a time to spoil the supper.

The fag himself had no time for a supper, for as soon as he had finished cooking he had to hunt around for knives and trenchers to be taken into Chambers for a late-night 'mess,' which his seniors would probably want. Having snatched these from departing diners in hall, he had to dash down to Chambers, sweep up, put on a fresh faggot, clean the grease from the candlesticks, and call out the quarter-hours for the benefit of any of his seniors who were present. As a reward for these labours he might sometimes be given a weak dilution of his prefect's tea; otherwise he had nothing at all.

At 7.30 p.m. there was lesson preparation, known as 'Toy-time' from the 'toy' (*i.e.* bureau) which each pupil had beside his bed.

'Almost all the fags' lessons,' says one Old Wykehamist, 'were learnt in Chambers at Toy-time, or sitting up in bed at night, as during two-thirds of the time in school they were merely repeating their lessons, and the fagging during the rest of the day was continuous.' The prefects in each Chamber sat at tables close to the fire, and the junior's studies might be interrupted by a prefect's desire to use him as a fire-screen. 'The living screen was obliged to keep continuously revolving, and to pull out his trousers from the more developed parts of his person, or he ran a risk of being scorched.'

Toy-time lasted for an hour and a half. Then the junior was free to perform his last duties of the day, once more cleaning the candlesticks, and then going to chapel.

The service finished, the junior was really on his last lap. The candles in Chambers had to be lit, and the toe-pans (foot-baths) filled. After this, his official duties were almost over.

If his lesson preparation had been inadequately covered during Toy-time, he might have to suppress his desire for sleep and continue his studies in bed. Otherwise, 'to bed and sleep now went the tired junior. But disturbance was still in store for him. The prefects sitting up might want the mess-towel, or fire-paper for a fresh faggot, and he was naturally roused to find them; or beer was required, and the nipperkin holding it was in his custody; or his snores demanded rough suppression; or it was thought that a bolster-match between two juniors would be an improving spectacle; or he was "launched" (the mattress and bedding pulled sharply to the ground) or "toefitied" (his big toe violently pulled with string).'

The Rev. W. Tuckwell records an even more dangerous disturbance of his bedtime rest by a prefect who was ordinarily kind enough but liable to outbursts of rage.

'I was sitting up in bed one night, doing Latin verse, while he was at his table. Something that I said angered him. He grasped the short heavy iron shovel in the fireplace and flung it at me with all his force. I ducked behind the mahogany writing-desk which stood beside me: the missile took off a corner of it as clean as by the stroke of a hatchet.'

Fagging was probably at its worst during the early half of the nineteenth century. After this the tendency was for abject slavery to diminish to simple servitude, and for the fag even to be allowed some time to himself.

None the less, the mid-Victorian or late-Victorian fag, at any rate in most public schools, was rarely allowed a *sense* of freedom, though he might in fact for the time being be free from any specific duty. Prefects at most schools were entitled at their whim to bellow for a fag in whatever jargon was customary at the school. (At Winchester they called for a 'Junior'; at Westminster they shouted 'Election'; Shrewsbury prefects demanded a 'Dowl.')

'By school law,' said (Sir) Michael Sadler, writing of Rugby (as ex-Captain of the School) in the 'eighties, 'the Sixth fellows may compel fags to do anything for them at any time . . . At the appointed times of breakfast, tea, and supper fagging is still a burden. A School House study does not provide sanctuary from the demands of the Sixth. Even there a fag must heed the loud voice of the Sixth fellow shouting for him; and he must leave letters, cooking, or *lessons* to answer the call. So small are some of the studies that to get out of them quickly is almost impossible; often a boy in his frantic haste will bring books, candles, and spirit-lamp in disastrous confusion to the floor.' This desperate hurry was easily explained. When the Sixth wanted anything, one of them went to the banisters and shouted 'F-a-a-g.' 'From all parts of the House, like rabbits from their burrows, rush the fags, and as the last man gets the work, they rush along as fast as they can.'

Westminster fags, like most others, had a lighter time at this period than they would have done forty or fifty years earlier. But every junior (first year scholar) had to fag, no matter in what Form, bar the Sixth, he was placed. Moreover, every senior (boy who had been more than three years in the school) had at least one fag. Anomalous situations obviously occurred at times, with boys in a low form fagging boys of their own age in a higher form. The fag's duties were to take the senior's boots and hot water to him in the mornings, and wake him, to call out the time for him if ordered, and carry his books into school. Any senior who wanted a fag could call for one at any time.

At Charterhouse fagging had grown milder by the 'eighties, but a fag was still liable to be sent on messages at almost any time by an 'upper.' At Winchester in the 'seventies, though fagging had shrunk to more tolerable proportions than in earlier years, it had not ceased to exist, nor were its penalties forgotten. 'If a cup was broken in getting tea ready, if a pot was left uncleaned, if balls were let pass while long-stopping at cricket—the ground-ash hung over the seat of the wretched junior.'

The principle remained steady for a great many years to come. Alec Waugh and a fellow prefect modified it a little at Sherborne during the First World War. The two shared eight fags between them. They appointed one of them fag-leader, instructing him that he would do no fagging himself, but that he must see to it that the others did their appointed tasks satisfactorily. If any of them failed, then *he*, the fag-leader, would be beaten. As late as the nineteen-thirties a fag at Harrow was automatically beaten if he failed to obey a call, dropped a tray, let a prefect's fire go out more than once a fortnight, or burnt a piece of toast more than once a week.

'Briefly,' says one modern apologist, 'fagging means the discharge of menial tasks by boys in their first terms for members of the Sixth Forms and monitors . . . It would appear that the thing that makes fagging tolerable, apart from the occasional hero-worship of one's master, is the ever-present hope that some day the fag too will be in the proud position of being able to yell for someone to do *his* bidding.' Strange as it may seem, this point is put forward in defence of the fagging system. But perhaps the most common and most foolish argument of all is that fagging knocks the conceit out of a boy. Only the most starry-eyed romantic can really believe that conceit is found more often among the youngsters who are compelled to do fagging than among the bloods and swells who compel them to do it.

At the present day, no doubt, fagging has become more sensible than it used to be. But the practice of bellowing for a fag whenever a prefect requires something to be done that he is too lazy to do for himself cannot really be justified. It may not be very bad for the junior, but it is exceedingly bad for the senior. On the other hand, it is reasonable for younger boys to be encouraged to *help* their seniors in certain specific ways at definite and limited times.

There is, indeed, a good case to be made out for training boys of all ages to develop the habit of performing courtesy services for older people. But the people who should most receive these services are the members of the staff, and those who should be most assiduous in performing them are the boys at the top of the school.

CHAPTER TEN

DIM RELIGIOUS LIGHT

RELIGION has had a varied and not always creditable school career.

In medieval times the Church, of course, controlled the schools, as it controlled most things. Many schools were directly connected with cathedrals or churches, teachers were often local clergymen, and the Bishop's licence to teach was a *sine qua non*.

The earliest pupils of Eton can have had little doubt that their school formed part of a Collegiate Church. 'Matins of the Blessed Virgin shall be said . . . by scholars in their dormitories while making their beds before five o'clock in the morning. Certain other prayers shall be said by the Usher and Scholars in School, and on the ringing of a bell, Scholars and Choristers shall alike repair to the Church,' where Mass and special Founder's prayers were said. Other prayers were said at intervals during the day until bedtime. It is worth remembering that Henry VI, a highly religious man if a most unsatisfactory king, intended the Eton Chapel to be larger than any cathedral in England except St Paul's.

The more enlightened educational thinkers of the Renaissance, such as Erasmus, Sir Thomas Elyot, and Roger Ascham, take a broader view of education, and are more concerned with teaching than with preaching and prayers. But religion began to assume a special political importance in Elizabethan times. If Catholic domination, recently thrown off after centuries of continuance, was to be kept firmly at bay, the schools would have to be used to foster and preserve the Protestant religion. Thus the many schools which had been founded for the furtherance of Roman Catholicism before the Reformation were subsequently used as a barrier against Catholic power; and thus the whirligig of time brings in its revenges.

Elizabethan Injunctions of 1559 laid down 'that all teachers of children shall stir and move them to live and do reverence to God's true religion now truly set forth by public authority,' that scriptural passages should be learnt by heart, and that children should be instructed by the clergy in the Ten Commandments and the Articles of Belief. At every grammar school, lessons began in the morning and ended at night with religious exercises, usually in the school-house, but sometimes in the parish church. Passages from the Scriptures 'or other goodly book' were supposed to be read during meals.

In these early times the sermon was no formality to be yawned through by bored scholars. 'As many as be of capacity do take in writing notes of the preacher's sermon, and give account of them on Monday morning to the Master.' This injunction of the Dronfield school statutes was a normal one. 'The very lowest,' says John Brinsley, 'can bring some notes, at least three or four.'

'Those who have been longer practised' have a stiffer task. First, Brinsley advocates, they should set down the text; secondly, they must set down every argument, with its proofs; thirdly, in the highest forms, they can give a complete summary and analysis of the sermon. As a finishing touch, 'You may, if you think good, cause them the next morning to translate it into good Latin style.'

No doubt all these provisions served their immediate purpose and played some part in helping to establish Protestant-ism as the State religion. But compulsory and automatic religious exercises, whatever the creed may be, soon lose their religious significance and become perfunctory. We find Brinsley, in 1612, recording regretfully of religious exercises that 'these are matters least thought of in most schools.'

Some of us, indeed, in a less religious-minded age, may feel that the one ray of sunshine percolating this bleak aspect of schoolboy life is that the solemn injunctions to read, mark, learn, inwardly digest, and outwardly latinize the preacher's prolixity were not always scrupulously insisted on. Simonds D'Ewes, at school at Bury St Edmunds during the second decade of the seventeenth century, looking back on his school-days from the unimaginative standpoint of serious adulthood, reproaches one of his masters for 'never causing his scholars to take notes of his sermons in writing, or so much as to repeat any one note they had learned out of them.'

Most schoolboys, even in early Stuart days, would take a less strait-laced view of their master's negligence; but D'Ewes was never a typical schoolboy. 'He neglected not only food sometimes but often his sleep for study,' we are told, 'and was rebuked, not for neglect of his book but often for sitting up too late at it.' I do not know whether the Stuarts had a word for him, but the modern schoolboy would certainly find one.

A service in the school chapel may be an impressive occasion, which can have at any rate a temporary influence on the boys who attend it. But there is a great deal of evidence that the general influence of these ceremonies has been vastly less than is supposed by some parents and some school chaplains. Boys whose daily visits to the chapel are automatic and often incon-venient see these things from an angle very different from that of the occasional visitor, transported by stained glass and pure treble voices.

Few things are more misleading than the angelic appearance of a choirboy, especially a school choirboy.

'We were all driven, much against our will,' says Edward Lockwood of Marlborough, 'fifteen times a week to chapel, where the singing made the service less irksome than it otherwise would have been. Had I not known the boys,' he adds, 'and watched their distorted faces while they sang, I might have imagined it came down direct from Heaven.'

The words of the psalms and anthems, at any rate, did not always come direct from Heaven. They were sometimes unprintable. Among the respectable variations was one which certain Eton boating enthusiasts used to import into the Hallelujah Chorus, based on the names of well-known Thames watermen.

'Jack Hatherley, Bob Tolladay,
Row all the day, Round Surley Bay,'
the solemn-looking worshippers would chant lustily.

It was at Eton, too, that rival performances of Psalm 136 were on one occasion given simultaneously. A school tradition was the raucous shouting by the whole school of the chorus to each verse, '*For His mercy endureth for ever,*' following the singing of the first part of the verse by the choir alone. The headmaster, Dr Hornby, at length came to regard this bellowing as unseemly, and conspired with the organist, the famous Dr Barnby, to defeat it by the introduction of a new chant, written for the occasion, which did not lend itself to musical excess.

At the initial performance the mass of boys were at first bewildered. Then, led by a common impulse, they began the familiar shout, disregarding the lead from the choir; and the two opposing versions of the psalm were given together, each trying to drown the other. Reinforcement was rushed to the support of the choir by the organist, who pulled out every stop in an effort to smother the unofficial rendering.

This 'most irreverent pandemonium,' as it was called by an ear-witness, occurred in the 'seventies, when the school choir was functioning strongly. A few years earlier the Hornby-Barnby plan could hardly have come into being, for there was no school choir. On Sunday mornings there was no music at all: at the afternoon service the choir of St George's Chapel, Windsor Castle, co-operated, but members had to leave half-way through the service to take part in their own Evensong.

This deficiency at Eton was not just a local one. At Harrow, for example, there was no singing by the boys until it was timidly introduced by Dr Christopher Wordsworth in the

Christ's Hospital Dining-Hall. Grace before dinner

late eighteen-thirties. The Fourth Form, consisting of about fifteen boys, led by the headmaster's wife 'in a tremulous voice,' piped out from the gallery one of Tate and Brady's psalms, while the rest of the school turned round and stared amazedly at the song-birds.

Until Wordsworth's time the school possessed no chapel of its own, but made use of the parish church. Even after the Harrow chapel was consecrated, the local Vicar, indignant at having his special congregation withdrawn and at seeing the headmaster (in Holy Orders, of course) rivalling his ecclesiastical activities, succeeded in bringing pressure to bear to compel the school to attend an afternoon service in the parish church as well as any other services which might be held in the school chapel.

Sunday was usually a day to be remembered, with the school chapel or local church occupying a solid portion of the pupil's waking hours, and with prayers and Bible readings in school filling in many of the gaps.

At Christ's Hospital the boys rose at seven—an hour later than usual—and after breakfast had a school service of psalms, hymns, and prayers. At 10.45 a.m. they went to church for a two-hour service. 'Our Bibles were very large, and we had to kneel during a considerable part of the service on hard boards, with no rest for our arms or heads. The misery of the Litany was beyond all words. At the end of it we little sinners were miserable enough.' After church the boys went at once to the dining-hall, where a lengthy service of Bible-reading, psalms, and prayers barred the way to dinner. At the end of the meal came an hour of Catechism-reciting and more Bible-reading. A bell was then rung, heralding the approach of another visit to the church, with the boys marching two by two.

Was there *any* time for recreation? Yes, indeed: Sunday, even at Christ's Hospital in the days of William IV, had its lighter side. On leaving the church the boys were permitted to take a short walk in the school playground. This concession to worldliness was followed by a long service in the dining-hall, after which came 'a cold and scanty' supper. Grace was said, and then the Master appeared to deliver the third sermon of the day. Now came bedtime, but this was not allowed to pass without a reminder to the boys that they were enjoying a holy day. A service, conducted by a monitor, took place in the dormitories. Finally the day was suitably rounded off by the chanting of the Burial Anthem.

Marlborough College had its own special Sunday penance. In the early days, although it was founded for sons of the clergy, it had no chapel of its own, and the pupils used to march to the parish church. 'There on Sundays we were put through a fearful ordeal which was called "being catechised," but which was really little better than a burlesque for the entertainment of outsiders and the college servants, who crowded into the gallery.'

Questioning would proceed on the following lines:

'What is the eighth commandment, boy?'

'Thou shalt not steal.'

'Do you ever pick or steal?'

'No, sir.'

'What! Do you never soil your clothes or books?'

The victim, timidly scenting a trap, would fail to answer, and the question would be sternly repeated.

'Sometimes,' the victim would at length admit.

'There!' the catechist exclaimed triumphantly. 'If you soil your clothes or books then you rob your parents and break the eighth commandment!'

Sunday was not a popular day at Marlborough.

At the Congregational School, Lewisham, the boys used to go twice a day to a small chapel at New Cross, where the head-master preached. The morning service included three hymns, a sermon, and one long prayer which lasted for fifteen or twenty minutes. During this prayer the old clerk chose the second hymn—a matter of some significance to the youthful congregation, for they had to learn it by heart when they returned to school. They also had to learn a passage from the

Bible and reproduce, from memory, the text and a general summary of the sermon. Punishment awaited them if they failed any of these Lord's Day tests. Some scripture was then read and explained, a hymn was sung, and the afternoon's proceedings concluded with prayers. In the evening a second visit was paid to the chapel at New Cross. 'The walk on dark winter nights was often past a joke, especially as we had at those times to encounter the hostility of the village lads.' Sometimes, in addition or as an alternative to evening chapel, the catechism was studied, learnt by heart, and tested.

It was the custom for the committee of governors occasionally to send round one or more of their members on a visit of inspection. A special sub-committee which examined the religious side of the school's arrangements in 1832 reported rather unfavourably—not because there were too many religious exercises for the pupils but because there were not enough.

The complaint could hardly have been made at Kingswood School, founded by John Wesley for educating the sons of dissenting ministers. The boys here, aged from eight to fourteen, were supervised continuously, the rule being that they were never to be out of the presence of a master, day or night, nor to go out of the school, even for a single day, until the moment of their final leaving. There were no holidays from work, and no time was allowed for play or recreation on any day. Every morning, winter and summer, they rose at four o'clock.

Brought up in these conditions, the boys were a ready prey to religious hysteria. 'On Wednesday,' a master reported joyfully to Wesley, 'God broke in among our boys in a surprising manner . . . the power of God came upon them, even like a mighty rushing wind, which made them cry aloud for mercy. Last night I hope will never be forgotten, when about twenty of the boys were in the uttermost distress. While I am writing, their cries, from their several apartments, are sounding in my ears.'

A year or two later, after the boys had been permitted the recreation of going in solemn procession to view the body of a neighbour and of listening to an even more solemn sermon, two of them, overcome by the occasion, began to cry aloud for mercy, 'and quickly another and another, till all but two or three were constrained to do the same.' After a few days of this, several of the boys became quite hoarse.

But religious enthusiasm in the young appears to be a transient emotion. 'There is scarce a trace of it remaining,' Wesley laments a year or two later.

In contrast to such religious orgies, the apathy of the ordinary schoolboy seems healthily agreeable. At Winchester, for example, young Tuckwell used to spend his time during service in the cathedral studying the bishop's throne, 'with its high canopy of intricate carved cusps and crotchets, and reflecting how easy and pleasant it would be to clamber to the topmost pinnacle.'

Certainly there was little in the services to inspire any kind of religious feeling. They were usually meaningless to their hearers, and sometimes the preacher was not even that. 'Sermons were so inaudibly delivered,' A. D. Coleridge reports in his *Eton in the 'Forties*, 'as to be, in some instances, little more than dumb show.' At Harrow the hour-long sermons were similarly profitless. The boys, placed in a distant gallery, could never hear a word of them.

'Worship there was literally none,' an Etonian of the 'seventies recorded. 'The sole thought was how to get the service over. Against the text of every anthem, in every anthem book, was written in pencil, corrected and tested by generations of impatient listeners, the time taken in its performance.' The most popular chaplain was the one 'whose fleetness in gabbling through the service at breakneck speed was phenomenal.'

In contrast, one of the dreariest moments at the same school was when Provost Goodford, in announcing a coming celebration of Holy Communion, instead of stopping at the usual place in the Exhortation, at the 65th word from the start, went on to read the remaining five hundred words to the pupils. 'His breath was scanty,' a future Eton headmaster recorded, 'and his voice was weak, so the performance was the reverse of edifying, especially as the congregation was standing and couldn't hear a word.'

This same Provost, though a kindly man, was a very lengthy preacher, and generations of Eton boys spent many weary hours half-listening to his almost inaudible discourses. Once, however, he knocked down his own wicket. It was the practice for the preacher, at the end of his sermon, to link it up with the next part of the service with the words, 'And now . . .' One day, only ten minutes after the start, and before he had even begun to get properly warmed up, the Provost inadvertently, after a slight pause, began a new sentence with the significant words, 'And now . . .' With a startled gasp of delight the whole congregation sprang to their feet, ready for the Offertory hymn, and the bewildered Provost found himself willy-nilly lopping a good sixty minutes off his sermon.

The common attitude of schoolboys to sermons was expressed by a verse published in the *Etonian* of 1875:

'At the magic words "And now,"
Runs a tremor through the hall.
Joy awakes on every brow,
Sleep is cast away from all.'

Of course, there have been exceptional preachers. Arnold's tremendous personality expressed itself in a type of pulpit discourse that was new in its day. He spoke intimately about ordinary everyday affairs in a tone of ardent sincerity. He was more preoccupied with a sense of sin that we today would appreciate. General feeling on these matters has changed, in some respects for the better, but not in all: Arnold and his contemporaries would probably be shocked, not to say contemptuous, of the way in which we have allowed ourselves to be duped by flabby psychological theories into the belief that a child's faults are never his own. To Arnold evil was something to be strongly opposed, not weakly excused; and he attacked it constantly in his sermons, so convincingly that even boys who too often failed to follow his precepts none the less, as one of them noted, 'used to listen to them from first to last with a kind of awe, and over and over again could not join my friends at the chapel door but would walk home alone.'

Few school sermons had so profound an effect. Many had no effect at all, being mumbled by old men who had no understanding of boys and no ability to reach their hearts even when they reached their ears. 'When the Fellows preached we slept or yawned.'

Arnold was in the habit of scribbling down his sermons almost immediately before delivery, even though the substance had been in his mind for some days. Thus every sermon was fresh and original. Not so the Fellows of Eton, some of whom used to preach the same dreary semi-inaudible discourses over and over again. One of them one afternoon found on the cushion of his pulpit a list of his very limited themes, together with the query: 'Which is it to be today?' Another at least made an effort to choose arousing texts: 'Shout!' was one text, and 'Wash!' was another. But the substance of his preaching was dreary enough, and the only occasion on which he really interested the boys was when a wasp found its way to the pulpit, and the preacher, who habitually used a reading-glass, appeared to the more distant members of his congregation to be playing a miniature game of rackets.

The habit of reading sermons was responsible for some odd performances, when the preachers made do with old material composed for some different occasion. 'The subject of my discourse this morning,' one doddering old Fellow informed his congregation of Eton boys, 'will be the duties of the married state.' Nor was the weakness always confined to the senile. At Winchester, for instance, the Rev. R. S. Barter, (the Warden), a great sportsman and a splendid character, used, like the rest, to read his sermons even in the decade that followed Arnold's retirement from Rugby. 'He constantly drew on old stores,' we are told, and one sermon—on the Witch of Endor—became quite a familiar friend to the boys. Perhaps it was more suited to their understanding than the sermon he preached on another occasion. Snatching up the first that came to hand before hurrying to chapel one evening he inadvertently failed to select one of his Winchester College sermons but instead seized one that he had formerly preached in his father's parish church. In due course 'he found himself presently exhorting the bewildered boys to bring their wives to Communion as soon as possible.'

The Winchester Cathedral canons, whose sermons helped to provide the boys with their Sunday morning religious edification, were, we are told (and by a clergyman), 'a queer lot.' One of them had a son at the school, who one day made a bet that he would make his father laugh in the pulpit. He won his wager.

Boys have often been driven to supply their own interest during sermon-time. At Lewisham the headmaster used to write the notes of his sermons in shorthand, and as he was so short-sighted that he had to wear two pairs of spectacles, he often came to a full stop while he tried to decipher his notes. He filled each pause with a series of grunts, and the boys used to count the grunts to see if he could break his record.

At Eton it has been recorded that dogs and squirrels were occasionally taken into the chapel to relieve the tedium. In Sir Osbert Sitwell's time an inoffensive boy sitting beside him was so overcome by the boredom of the service that he drew from his pocket a box of fusees (the brightly glowing, slow-burning matches used for igniting hand-grenades) and threw it with great force into the middle of the aisle. It burst into flames, and was at length removed by the Verger with a pair of tongs. The culprit was sternly denounced from the pulpit as a boy who had disgraced himself (presumably in ascending order of values) as a Christian, a gentleman, and an Etonian.

*   *   *

I do not think anyone would deny that a school ought to try to exert a good moral influence on its pupils. But when we come to consider the part that religion has played and should play in this desirable attempt, we find ourselves on very slippery ground. Educational history shows that formal religion has rarely had the effect that its most zealous exponents are eager to claim for it. It is perhaps worth considering that dissipation and brutality were never more rife in our schools than when most of the staff were clerics. (The Canon from Surrey who wrote, quite recently, to a national newspaper, demanding that all teachers should be submitted to religious tests, should ponder for a long while over this disillusioning fact.)

Whatever our religious views may be, I think most of us would agree that children should at least have some familiarity with those Christian ideas and Biblical narratives which have contributed so much to Western culture. (Some of us would go further, and try to make them aware, too, of some other great religions.) But all of us, and especially ardent churchmen, must beware of being too ready to blame the non-sectarianism of the State schools for any current growth in crime or for any startling exhibition of religious ignorance. No evidence has ever been offered to show that Church schools produce better citizens and nobler men than State schools; and a study of school life certainly fails to show any convenient coincidence between attendance at religious services and virtuous conduct. Virtue and true religion are both nearer to the heart than to the mouth.

As for ignorance, like the wind it bloweth where it listeth; and it does not always alight in non-sectarian State schools.

Few of us, I suppose, would wish to return to the persistent religious devotions that produced in D'Arcy Thompson, at Christ's Hospital, 'my Sunday evening feeling of blank, cold, hungry, church-wearied, sermon-stunned, for-ever-and-for-everish despair.' But most of us would probably deplore the religious ignorance of the ten-year-old boy called to give evidence in a fairly recent motoring case, and handed a copy of the Bible with which to take the oath. For the sequel I quote exactly from the report given in *The Daily Telegraph*.

> Do you know what that book is you are holding?—No.
> Have you ever heard of the Bible?—No.
> Have you ever heard of God?—No.
> Do you know anything about Jesus Christ?—No.

As I write I can almost hear the thunderous cries of 'I told you so' from those eager churchmen who have been most vociferous in condemning the 'godless' State schools. In my mind's eye I see a worthy Canon reaching impetuously for his pen and notepaper that he may indite an even more indignant demand for a return to the good old days of a religious inquisition for all teachers. But stay, good Canon, before you put pen to paper. Let us first ascertain the nature of this ungodly place of learning.

I will quote again from the report:

'He is a pupil of St A—— School, a Roman Catholic School.'

CHAPTER ELEVEN

A BREATHLESS HUSH IN THE CLOSE

IT is probably significant that the best-known statement on English education is connected with Sport. Ask any person you meet in the street where the Battle of Waterloo was won, and if the word 'playing-fields' is not out of his mouth before the question is finished you may be sure that he is of foreign extraction. The familiar Wellington epigram has egged on thousands of prefects to beat their juniors for not playing in or supporting House cricket and football matches; it has encouraged hundreds of thousands of spectators at Lord's and Wembley to believe that they are in some way contributing to the national welfare; and it is no doubt partly responsible for the enthusiasm with which the weekly football pool is conducted in a million homes.

It is, therefore, a little unfortunate that Arthur Wellesley never made the remark attributed to him, and that if he ever said anything like it, he had neither cricket nor football in mind and was in no way referring to the team spirit. To him the playing-fields of Eton were the open spaces where he and his companions played hide-and-seek and ditch-jumping.

It is on record that he visited the College some three years after the defeat of Napoleon, and looked over the dame's boarding-house where he had lived nearly forty years earlier. In the big garden at the back of the house he smiled reminiscently. 'I really believe,' he remarked, 'that I owe my spirit of enterprise to the tricks I used to play in this garden.' That casual comment is the basis of the epigram which has driven so many children to compulsory games on carefully laid-out football and cricket pitches.

Those sportsmen who have long pictured the future Duke of Wellington learning to be a leader by captaining a victorious cricket team on Agar's Plough have, alas, been kidding themselves. And there is another great military figure whose school career was disillusioning. Baden-Powell was never captain of anything at Charterhouse. 'Cricket? Football? Yes, I enjoyed them, but they died long ago, they are only a memory, like much that I learnt at school. It was in the copse that I gained most of what helped me in after life . . .'

But we must not speak disrespectfully of Sport, which in due course was to become the core of English education, especially in the public schools.

'I remember,' says Alec Waugh, speaking of Sherborne in the First World War, 'a Housemaster once saying that it was impossible for a member of the House side to do much work while the House matches were in progress. And as the House matches covered a period of six weeks, this was a pretty generous allowance.' Small wonder that Waugh, himself no mean cricketer, considered that the boys could think of little else but sport; and in *The Loom of Youth* he gave a realistic impression, hot from experience, of the games cult at its most feverish. Sherborne certainly carried athletic fanaticism as far as it could go. A grim House Cricket match in 1926 lasted for six days.

Athlete worship was by no means a new thing in the early decades of this century. At Clifton, for example, in the 'eighties, the College succeeded in defeating its great county rival, Cheltenham, at cricket—the sixth victory, after three defeats and three draws. The game was played away; and when the victorious team returned to Clifton in their horse-drawn coach they found that the news of their triumph had somehow preceded them. They were met near the College by the sergeant, a first swallow of the coming summer. 'They are all waiting for you,' he announced, saluting. A little further on, the head of the school and another prefect were standing near a corner to prepare the way for the homecoming.

'Stop at the corner and take the horses out,' the head prefect told the driver.

As they turned the corner, the team saw the assembled school ready to pay homage. A phalanx of boys, fifteen deep, stretched right across the wide road—over six hundred of them. One tremendous yell burst from their throats at the sight of the coach, and then an outburst of continuous cheering went on for many minutes. The name of each member of the team was shouted and lustily cheered. Even the scorer was similarly greeted—unjustly, let us hope—as one who had done his bit towards victory.

The team cheered back; the horses were taken out; and a mass of boys surged round the coach. It was pushed towards the school like a battering ram; and indeed the proceedings somewhat resembled an act of war. Several boys were knocked down, three were seriously hurt, and even the headmaster was lucky to escape being trampled on. Close to the school the head prefect made a rush at Brain, the victorious captain, 'with a yell like a gorilla, and caught him by the leg. Before Brain could say "Jack," about a hundred fellows had him, and they carried him into his garden in Pembroke Road, yelling all the way.'

The captain of a cricket team, even as early as the 'seventies, was by far the most important person in a games-loving school such as Harrow. One summer this distinguished person, in a fit of sulks, announced his decision not to play at Lord's. The school was thrown into rather more consternation than if the staff had announced their intention to go on strike for more pay. 'Will it be believed,' cries an Old Harrovian, 'that a great headmaster, such as Dr H. M. Butler, should have entreated his pupil to play?' It will, in fact, be readily believed by anyone who has studied the effect of games on the boys and staff of an average school. In this instance 'the headmaster's prayer was granted, the sulky boy consented to play, and the reputation of the school was saved.'

Harrow was one of the schools where successful athletes,

as a matter of course, farmed out their academic exercises on those nonentities whose feeble claim to existence was an ability to do Latin and Greek or perhaps (in later years) Maths. C. H. P. Mayo, a popular Harrow master of the late nineteenth century, records that one big boy, more advanced in cricket than in Latin composition or mathematical calculations, used to go round regularly every Saturday evening with a bag containing slips of paper. 'On one was written Latin Prose; on another Algebra, or another Geometry. He made the scholars each draw a slip. The one who drew Prose had to do the athlete's prose for the coming week, and so on.' Alec Waugh refers to a similar type of exploitation at Sherborne.

One can understand the athlete's point of view: 'I win honour for the House and School by my sporting ability and the scholars must do their share too.' That is typical enough schoolboy logic, and one expects a young athlete to be so obsessed by his own little world as to see no further than its borders. But the most interesting and significant thing about this affair is Mayo's own attitude. 'The athlete's argument,' he comments, with all the fervour of a third-former, 'was very sound.' The schoolmaster, it is sometimes said scathingly, is a man among boys and a boy among men. What the scoffer has failed to realise is that the schoolmaster is too often a boy among boys.

Games worship was less universal in the 'seventies and 'eighties than it became later; and before the middle of the century it existed mainly at Harrow. At Shrewsbury, for example, Dr Samuel Butler had tacitly accepted cricket; but he left it to the boys to amuse themselves at it in their own way, and had less than little sympathy for other sports. Boating and football were forbidden, the former because of the danger of drowning, the second because he considered it 'only fit for butcher boys.' His successor, Dr Kennedy (whose Primer dominated the lives of several generations of young Latinists), legalised the game and in general was tolerant towards sport, but he was determined that games should be kept in their place. He had been an assistant master at Harrow, where he found cricket and football 'so zealously pursued and with such organisation of the whole school that it is vain to expect anything like extensive reading and sound scholarship.'

Even at Harrow, cricket and football at this period were far from being the exclusive sports that they subsequently became at most public schools; while at Eton they shared favour with pastimes that a prep school would nowadays blush to be discovered playing. Spinning tops was a highly popular Eton game in the 'forties. 'The schoolyard, before lessons began, was humming all over with peg-tops, and he who could split his comrade's plaything into two halves at the first fling was voted an expert.' Marbles was popular as late as 1821. Earlier still, the school that prided itself on its rather blasé superiority was buzzing with boys playing hopscotch, puss in the corner, kites, humming-tops, hunt the hare, and battledore, not to mention such less familiar activities as bally cally, peg in the ring, conquering lobs, steal baggage, cut gallows, chuck, sinks, stare caps, and hustlecap. The names are taken from a list made out in 1762; and it is interesting to note that cricket, fives, and football are included among these less exalted sports without any suggestion that they are on a different level.

Playing with hoops was also a favourite activity in many public and grammar schools. 'Hoops' occurs in the list just mentioned (between 'conquering lobs' and 'marbles'); and it is perhaps worth while to correct those readers of Gray's *Ode on a Distant Prospect of Eton College* who visualise the boy 'chasing the rolling circle's speed' as an out-fielder gallantly saving a boundary or a footballer dashing down the sideline with the ball at his feet. The 'circle' was nothing more than a wooden hoop. As late as 1805 the Duke of Richmond, at Westminster, gave a thrashing to another boy who had thrown the Duke's hoop over a wall. Even in the eighteen-twenties the October half at Eton was described by a contemporary as 'hoop time' for all except the seniors. At Hertford Grammar School in the eighteen-thirties a popular game was 'turnpikes with hoops.' The turnpikes were two bricks placed a foot apart through which the hoop had to pass without touching: if the driver failed he had to take the place of the turnpike keeper.

The hoop now seems to have passed out of existence. They were common in the first two decades of this century, and I often trundled one (an iron one: wooden hoops were for girls) along the pavements of my London suburb. But this was in my younger childhood, and I find it as difficult to picture myself chasing the rolling circle's speed around the playground of my minor public-school as to imagine myself giving my awe-inspiring headmaster a smack on the back. I can remember in my first term at the school being contemptuously rebuked by a dignified prefect for playing 'conkers' with a form-mate. What would he have said, I wonder, to puss in the corner or hopscotch?

It would be wrong to infer from all this that the schoolboy of earlier centuries was a namby-pamby who followed childish pursuits through fear of being hurt at more manly sports. It is merely the attitude to games that has changed. The eighteenth-century schoolboy amused himself in any way that occurred to him, whether it chanced to be cricket, catch-ball, or bally cally. Snobbery, prevalent enough in other fields, had not yet found its way to the school playing-field.

In the sixteenth century sport played a small part in the scholar's somewhat arduous twelve-hour day. Holidays, as we have seen, were only occasional, and games were often limited by statute. In 1571 John Lyon confined the pupils of his Harrow foundation to Tops, Running, Archery, and Tossing a Handball. The statutes of Shrewsbury School, founded in 1552, laid down that 'the scholars' play shall be shooting in the long bow and chess play, and no other games unless it be running, wrestling, or leaping.'

By the following century the schoolboy's natural tendency to seek amusement had become more readily recognised, or at any rate less vigorously subdued. In addition to the now

orthodox sports of cricket, hockey, and fives, and such mild
pursuits as diabolo and bandalore, common outlets for boys'
primitive energies were discovered in rough and sometimes
brutal field sports. Cudgelling was popular, and even so
innocent-seeming a pastime as hoop-rolling had its sharper
side. 'Some pretty hard blows arise,' we are told, from hoop
skirmishes; at one period it was the custom for two large
sides of Collegers and Oppidans at Eton, each armed with heavy
hoop-sticks as weapons and gowns as shields, to meet in the
Long Walk for a trial of strength.

Hunting, in one form or another, was an activity much
favoured by many boys. An Eton speciality was the 'Ram-
Hunt,' which was first carried out about 1687. The ram was let
loose, chased across fields and through hedges by boys armed
with clubs, and at length battered to death. The young Duke of
Cumberland, aged nine, paid a special visit to Eton one day
in 1730 to take part in this eighteenth-century frolic. He was
formally presented with a ram-club by the captain of the
school, and was invited to strike the first blow, which apparently
he did readily enough. He was also in at the kill, and 'blooded'
according to custom. Later in life he became known as Butcher
Cumberland, with Scots instead of rams to bludgeon and hack.

This sport for budding butchers lasted for about eighty
years, with one important modification. A ram one day
crossed the Thames and ran through the market-place at
Windsor with young hunters in full cry after it. The tender
hearts of Eton educationists were touched—on behalf of the
boys. Such violent exercise, it was thought, could not be good
for them, so in subsequent years the actual chase was abandoned:
the ram was ham-strung to prevent it from running away,
and the boys gathered round it in Weston's Yard and beat it
to death with their clubs as it lay helpless on the ground.
The 'sport' eventually came to be regarded as rather barbarous
even by eighteenth-century Etonians, and was abolished in
1747.

More orthodox hunting was carried out at some schools, and

H

irregular poaching at many more. A pack of beagles was kept at Eton, from the eighteenth century onwards. Though it was stopped by the authorities from time to time, by 1865 it had achieved recognition, and was carried on without any interruption, and the runs were duly recorded in the *Eton Chronicle*. At Rugby beagling was put down by Dr Arnold, an action defended by 'Old Brooke' against the sportsmen of the school.

Harrow, too, had its beagles, at any rate in the early nineteenth century, in spite of opposition by the school authorities. They were kept in a cottage pigsty at a village near by. On hunting days the keeper brought them unobtrusively, two at a time, to the meeting-place. The meet usually took place after hours, and the hunters let themselves down from the windows by ropes.

At Winchester in the eighteen-forties there was often a badger hunt during the school's thrice-weekly compulsory exercising on St Catherine's Hill, particularly in the winter. The prefects and some of their favoured protégés brought the wretched animal out in a sack, headed it towards the downs, and chased it, sometimes as far as ten miles out and back again. If the badger sought refuge in a hole it was driven out with dogs.

This was an unkind enough sport, but less brutal than the 'boar-hunting' which took place at least once at Shrewsbury in Dr Butler's day. Some members of his Sixth Form, after reading an account of a boar hunt in the *Iliad*, decided to have a hunt of their own in imitation. Lacking an authentic boar they used the pigs of a neighbouring farmer, releasing them from the sty for the purpose. The angry farmer, not a student of Homer, paid an immediate visit to the headmaster. One of the culprits, however, forestalled him. Disguising himself as the Doctor in a cap and gown, he met the farmer at the gate, listened to his story, and gravely promised to flog the offenders.

The story would be an entertaining one if it were not that the hunt was in fact, in a contemporary's words, 'most brutal and disgraceful.' However, Dr Butler when he heard of the affair—related in Latin verse—was so delighted that, according to one of the hunters, he gave the Sixth a half-holiday. It seems incongruous in the circumstances that he should have objected to football as only fit for butcher boys.

When Marlborough College was first established in the 'forties, hunting, trapping, and poaching in their crudest forms were the only outside activity of the pupils. The complete absence of organised games was in keeping with the complete absence of any other form of organisation, but it was felt far less by the boys than the lack of general supervision, for most of them were country-bred boys more familiar with the cruelties of the open field than with disciplined team games. Some boys kept ferrets, looked after by local cottagers or inn-keepers. Bird-nesting was, of course, a regular pastime.

An implement much used at this period was a 'squaler'— a pear-shaped piece of lead attached to a handle about eighteen inches long. It could be thrown with terrific force and was as deadly as a bullet. It was supposed to be used for squirrel hunting, but rabbits and hares also felt its weight. Indeed, even deer-stealing was practised by daring boys, deerskins being valuable. Some boys became accomplished skinners, not always to their own profit in so lawless a community. The official historian of the College relates how a friend of his, when at Marlborough, was caught on the downs by two big deer-killers, and made to skin the dead animal while they hurried back for call-over. He was severely punished for being late, but presumably preferred the restricted official punishment to the unrestricted maltreatment of his seniors.

The march of progress cannot be halted; and the day was approaching when recognised team games were to be almost openly accepted as the basis of an Englishman's education. By the beginning of this century it was pretty well established that a boy's classical misdemeanours could always be forgiven if his cricket was sound; and, conversely, that no kind of brilliance in French or History could really excuse feebleness at football or hockey.

The recognised public school games can more or less be ranked according to their generally accepted significance, though the ranking would not, perhaps, be universally approved even in the public schools themselves, still less in their imitators.

Cricket, without question, has always been the leading sport in the leading schools, partly because it is older—as an inter-school game—than football, partly because of its grace and elegance, and partly because footballers, even when the game became respectable, could not agree among themselves whether to use their hands or their feet, and whether to dash down the field or butt their heads against a wall. 'Ten to make and the match to win' remains the apotheosis of Everyman's vision of the public schools.

Next to cricket, I suppose, must come rowing, because only the luckier and more exclusive schools could afford the luxury of a boathouse on a convenient river. The Captain of the Boats at Eton has traditionally been a more important person than the football captain. Rugby football and Association football (in that order) must be regarded as next in importance, however. Rackets, squash rackets, fives and fencing are more exclusively typical of the public schools, even today, but they touch only the few. Vastly more Old Boys have come under the influence of Rugger. Hockey has had its following, but the game has not, on the whole, made the same impact on schoolboys as football. None the less, at Tonbridge in the eighteen-forties it was the favourite autumn game, the players cutting their own sticks in the neighbouring woods (to the annoyance and often despite the interference of the property owner) and then steaming them to the required shape. Athletics, of course, is a sport as universal as cricket, but it would be idle to pretend that it is regarded with the same feeling as a cricket or football match against a particular rival, probably because even the best organisation cannot make Sports Day anything but a series of spasmodic incidents.

Fifty years ago *Whitaker's Almanack* lamented that talent

among the younger players of lawn tennis would not be easily
found 'until the public schools adopt a more favourable
attitude towards the game.' Even today, it has to fight for
a footing against the dominance of cricket. It is perhaps
ironical that the first specific reference to any school game
is not to cricket but to a relative of its humble summer rival.
A phrase book published in 1519 by the former Master of
Eton (a Wykehamist) contains the revealing sentence, 'He hit
me in the eye with a tennis ball.' This precedes by eighty years
the earliest known mention of cricket—an entry in one of the
Guildford Corporation records. A gentleman of the town,
called to give evidence in a dispute over a plot of land, stated
that when he was a boy at the Free (Grammar) School he
and his companions 'did runne and plaie there at crickett and
other plaies'; and since nobody apparently demanded an
explanation of 'crickett' the game must have been popular,
at any rate in this part of the greatest cricketing county, in
the first half of the sixteenth century.

But our business here is not with the origins of rival sports
but with their school significance. Cricket, although quite
popular among a host of other schoolboy games, did not
begin to assume definite leadership until the beginning of
the nineteenth century. In the previous century it had often
had to fight for mere existence. At Westminster in 1744 it had
to do this quite literally, for the right of play on Tuttle Fields
was disputed by a group of local youths, who seemingly had a
club of their own.

An account of the trouble was given to an absent friend
by one of the school cricketers, aged about fifteen.

'I don't doubt but you have heard of the quarrel we have
had with the Westminster Club . . . Last Tuesday night they
took our place, who as soon as we came into the fields turn'd
'em out, they being, I am sure, at least a hundred, and all our
boys were not in the fields. One of them immediately knocked
down Kavannah, another Richard Cooper, which broke his
bat, then they all surrounded us and drove us quite out of the

fields. Not content with that they came into Dean's Yard
arm'd with Hangars and bats and swore they'd kill the first
boy they met.'

In spite of such violent opposition, cricket managed to
flourish at Westminster. The first public school cricket match
was a contest in 1796 between Westminster and Eton on a
neutral ground at Hounslow Heath. But cricket, even at the
close of the century, was still not quite a recognised sport,
especially at Eton. The match was a stolen entertainment,
frowned on by Dr Heath. He had in fact refused the Eleven
leave to play in it; and although it took place in the last week
of the summer term and most of the team were about to leave
school, they were all flogged after the game.

Better times, however, were on the way. In the new century,
under a new headmaster, cricket was soon accepted as a
recognised Eton ceremony. In 1808 the Eleven played the
M.C.C., then a club of twenty years' standing. Far from
punishing the participants, Dr Goodall patronised the match,
and gave particular praise to one boy, Sir Christopher
Willoughby, who was apparently the school Bailey of his day.

The headmaster's geniality is perhaps more to be commended
than his cricketing judgement. 'This boy,' says a contemporary
record, 'by a system of beautiful blocking wearied out the
skill and even the patience of his adversaries. He could stay
in for the greater part of an innings without ever making
more than a single run at a time, and with a small score at the
end.'

'Such a style of play,' Maxwell Lyte commented, writing in
the days of Grace, Ranjitsinhji, Maclaren, and Jessop, 'would
hardly be considered interesting nowadays.' The whirligig
of time brings repetition as well as revenges, and today
Willoughby would doubtless be considered the ideal man to
open an England Test innings.

Another indication of the slowly dawning official acceptance
of sport as an essential part of school life was the enclosure by
Dean Vincent, also in 1808, of ten acres of Tuttle Fields to

form a playing-field for Westminster scholars. By this time they had stopped playing Eton at cricket, and ten years later were showing the first signs of that ugly snobbery which sport has unfortunately helped to develop in the public schools. A note in the Westminster cricket ledger for 1818 reads:

'A challenge was sent to us by the Charterhouse to play them at cricket, which was very properly refused, not only on account of their being such inferior players, but it was thought beneath Westminster to receive a challenge from a private school.'

In spite of the supercilious tone of this entry, Westminster, it seems, were not playing any school matches at this time. In 1799 and the two following years they had renewed the Eton fixture, drawing one match and losing the others, after which they played no more school matches until 1850. The opponent on this occasion, ironically, was Charterhouse; and the Charterhouse match, ever since, has become one of the chief annual fixtures. Still more ironically, Westminster, on the admission of one of their chief cricketing exponents, 'have rarely been able to defeat their old opponent.'

By the eighteen-thirties cricket was in full swing at many schools, though it was still a pupil-activity: the obsessed games master and the feverish games cult were as yet future evils. Other evils, however, were not wanting in these days when to be big and strong was to be lord of a host of slaves.

One of the many miseries of the Winchester junior was to be caught up in the activity known as 'Watching out,' which meant fielding the ball either in front of the wicket or as long-stop (there were no nets) while a series of hefty seniors batted and bowled. Many a youngster today would be proud and happy to act as fieldsman for the benefit of a leading member of the School Eleven. But the activity would be voluntary and limited. In earlier days it was never voluntary and rarely limited.

'I have been, on a Saint's day [a holiday] ordered down to the Meads early in the morning before breakfast, and not allowed to quit the ground (except to attend chapel) till dark, the whole time without a hat, often in the broiling sun. At breakfast time and at one o'clock one of the fags would be sent up to bring down food, which we ate on the ground.' To add to the injustice of this forced labour, the victim was quite likely to be given an imposition for shirking compulsory exercise on St Catherine's Hill.

'We "watched out" bareheaded,' writes another Wykehamist of the period. 'I have felt my hair so hot as to be painful to the touch, and have seen the heads of other juniors steaming in the sun. At last a boy called Lewis was struck down with brain fever after several hours of this sport, and fags were then allowed to wear hats.'

None the less, the other pains of 'watching out' remained, and were especially bitter to the young child to whom a powerfully hit ball was as alarming as a cannon ball.

'The first time one came my way,' wrote the Rev. W. Tuckwell, 'I deftly let it pass and ran after it. I can hear today (fifty years after) the strident, high-pitched voice of V. C. Smith, the Captain of the Eleven, whose bat had propelled it.

' "Fetch up that ball and then come here."

'I stood before Smith, a big strong boy of nineteen or twenty.

' "Why did you shirk that ball?"—and as he spoke he gave me a box on the ear that knocked me down and left the glands swollen and painful for days. I have seen a stump laid heavily on the loins of a little boy for the same offence.'

The Wykehamist first quoted supports the evidence, mentioning the case of a big prefect over twenty years old putting a young boy about ten paces behind the wicket, pointing to a spare stump, and saying with a scowl: 'You see that stump? The first ball you miss I'll cut you in three pieces— body, soul, and legs.'

No doubt this approach was an encouragement to good fielding; but in the circumstances a holiday was not always looked forward to by the younger pupils at Winchester.

SMYTH.

Football at Rugby in 1845

At Eton, boys below the Fifth forms had to field or bowl to the Seniors whenever the latter so decreed. As the Fifth used to station themselves at every exit when the lower boys were coming from the schoolroom the chances of escape were small. There was, however, an opportunity for an older boy to show a little knightly chivalry, for a gracious custom existed whereby a Fifth former who caught a batsman out was entitled to set free any fag who happened to be beside him.

Even at Marlborough in the 'fifties, though organised games had only just been introduced, the traditional evils were at once incorporated with the benefits. A fag caught early in the day frequently found himself doomed to spend the rest of his holiday in fielding for his seniors' convenience.

The man who first thought of cricket nets should have a statue erected to his memory on every public school playing-field.

Akin to the practice of 'watching out' at cricket was the custom of 'kicking in' at football. There were no white-painted side-lines at Winchester in the 'thirties and 'forties. The lines were formed by two long rows of unfortunate juniors—gownless and in their waistcoats, however bitter the winter winds—who had to stand exactly in line, five or six yards apart, each boy ready to kick the ball back into play if the ball came near him or retrieve it if it passed over him, and possibly to be kicked or struck by an ill-tempered senior who regarded himself as having been robbed of the ball. Another junior stood at each end in the centre of what today would be called the goal-line. His function, however, was not to act as goal-keeper but to act as goal. He stood with his legs apart and a rolled-up gown at each foot. If the ball passed between his legs or over his head three points were scored; two points were awarded for a shot that passed over one of the gowns, and one for a shot that passed outside the gown.

In rather bitter contrast to the shivering fags who formed the touch-line, the characteristic of the Winchester game was what was known as a 'hot,' which seems to have been something

like a modern Rugger scrum with no particular rules to hamper
the players from attacking each other. 'The game is fierce
enough after its own fashion,' writes a chronicler of the 'sixties
casually, 'a broken leg being no rare occurrence during the
season.' A Wykehamist of the 'forties is even more emphatic.
'It was a tremendous exhibition of skill and savagery, one or
more maimed boys being habitually carried off in the course
of it to the sick-house, and their places taken by others. I
remember an old Peninsular officer witnessing a "six and six"
(six a side), and telling us that he would rather charge a French
regiment than go into a Winchester "hot." '

Twenty-two a side was often played at Winchester, but six
a side was more popular with the connoisseur. Here the game
differed from the Rugby School game, where the bigger the
'maul' the better it was appreciated. Readers of the most famous
football match in fictional history will recall that the whole
school took part in the game, a full three hundred, and that
much of the play consisted in a huge mass of players pushing
and hacking each other: 'You can see nothing for minutes
but a swaying crowd of boys.' That is a maul; and we are not
surprised to learn that, according to East, 'there's been two
collar-bones broken this half, and a dozen fellows lamed;
and last year a fellow had his leg broken.' It is, however,
reassuring to learn that the rules of Rugby School football,
as amended in the 'sixties, laid it down that 'Though it is lawful
to hold any player in a maul, this holding does not include
attempts to throttle or strangle.'

Another feature of the game at this school was the uneven
matching of sides. In Tom Brown's great game, fifty or sixty
School House boys, some of them quite small, were matched
against the remaining 250 members of the school. A few years
later, when school numbers had been allowed to swell, the forty-
five members of the Sixth used to face a mass of opponents
numbering up to 450—a contest which, we are told, was
notorious for vicious play. At one time, before Arnold's
day, it was customary for the twelve senior members of the

Sixth to challenge and defeat the rest of the school; but the 'play' was so ferocious and dangerous that the headmaster had to forbid the match.

Subsequent headmasters raised no objections to the fury of the normal game. Dr Arnold, it will be remembered, patronised the great School House match with his friendly interest, though it remained a game *for* the boys organised *by* the boys. Dr Temple, his successor, was even more detached in his interest. An Old Rugbeian wrote that his father was one day watching a game by Dr Temple's side and commenting on a scrimmage in which the boys seemed inextricably mixed up.

'Do you ever stop this sort of thing?' he inquired.

'Never, short of manslaughter,' replied Dr Temple.

The sheer intensity of feeling that goes into any school game, but especially on the football field and the cricket pitch, is probably responsible for the familiar belief that no period of life is so happy as the schoolboy's. Perhaps it is true that nothing can equal, for sheer ecstasy, the emotions of the boy who has scored a dashing try in an important House match, or reached a century against his school's chief rival. We must, however, remember that these achievements are but fleeting moments in the brief lives of a handful of schoolboy heroes. The rank and file are more familiar with the fumbled pass and the dropped catch in a minor game on an outer playing-field.

It is after all just as well, when we come to think of it, that happiness is not the special prerogative of the schoolboy. It would be a sad thing if life really reached its peak at the age of eighteen. It does, indeed, for a few sporting 'bloods,' and the rest of their days are spent in a pathetic anticlimax.

For most of us, happily, life holds more in store than a handful of ecstatic moments—and a host of grim ones—on the school playing-field. Even sport itself becomes more pleasurable as it grows less feverishly intense.

'In the long run,' wrote Alec Waugh a few years after leaving Sherborne, where he was a pillar of the School cricket team, 'I find cricket more enjoyable today than I did six years ago . . . One can field out all day and never take a wicket, miss a couple of catches, and then crown everything by making a duck, and yet thoroughly enjoy oneself. At school that would have been a rotten day, and one would have spent the evening in deep despondency.'

A breathless hush in the close when there's the match to win is one thing; but a deathly hush in the common room when the match has been lost by a bad stroke or a bungled catch is quite another matter.

VALETE

When I went up for the last of my six prizes, Doctor Arnold stood up and said: 'Stanley, I have now given you from this place every prize that can be given, and I cannot let it pass without thanking you thus publicly for the honour you have reflected upon the school.' The applause was great, and so ended my Rugby career with the most glorious hour I have ever had.

ARTHUR PENRHYN STANLEY
(Rugby, 1829–1834)

I bear in mind well with how prodigal a hand prizes used to be showered about; but I never got a prize. From the first to the last there was nothing satisfactory in my school career— except the way in which I licked the boy who had to be taken home to be cured.

ANTHONY TROLLOPE
(Winchester and Harrow,
1822–1834)

I cannot say that I look back upon my life at a public school with any sensations of pleasure, or that any earthly considerations would induce me to go through my years there again.

LEWIS CARROLL
(Rugby, 1846–1849)

I am excessively glad I came here, for I think I may say without boasting that I have found out more of the proportions of things . . . But

I am excessively glad that I am leaving. I hate the place and almost all its associations.

JAMES ELROY FLECKER
(Uppingham, 1901–1902)

I have two recurring nightmares, and one of them (happily less frequent in recent years) is dreaming that I am back at school again.

SPIKE HUGHES
(Perse)

BIBLIOGRAPHY

ASCHAM, ROGER, *The Scholemaster*, 1570.

AUBREY, JOHN (1626–1697), *Brief Lives*, ed. by Anthony Powell, 1949.

BADLEY, J. H., *A Schoolmaster's Testament*, 1937.

BAINES, J. M. and CONISBEE, L. R., *The History of Hastings Grammar School*, 1956.

BALLANTINE, WILLIAM, *Some Experiences of a Barrister's Life*, 1882.

BARNARD, H. C., *A Short History of Education* (1760–1944).

BLACKBURN, FRED, *George Tomlinson*, 1954.

BLUNDEN, EDMUND, *Christ's Hospital*, 1923.

BOSWELL, JAMES, *Life of Samuel Johnson* (1709–84), 1791.

BRADLEY, A. G., and Others, *A History of Marlborough College* (Revised), 1923.

BRINSLEY-RICHARDS, J., *Seven Years at Eton* (1857–64), 1883.

BROWN, J. H., *Elizabethan Schooldays*, 1933.

BRYANT, P. H. M., *Harrow* (*English Public Schools*), 1937.

BUTLER, SAMUEL, *Life and Letters of Dr Samuel Butler*, 1896.

CARLETON, J. D., *Westminster* (*English Public Schools*), 1938.

CARLISLE, NICHOLAS, *A Concise Description of the Endowed Grammar Schools in England and Wales*, 1818.

CARROLL, LEWIS, *Life and Letters*, by S. D. Collingwood, 1898.

CECIL, VISCOUNT, OF CHELWOOD, *All the Way*, 1949.

CHRIST'S HOSPITAL BOOK, THE, 1953.

COLERIDGE, A. D., *Eton in the 'Forties*, 1896.

COLERIDGE, HON. GILBERT, *Eton in the Seventies*, 1912.

COLLINS, W. LUCAS, *Etoniana*, 1865.

COLLINS, W. LUCAS, *The Public Schools*, 1867.

COOPER, THOMAS, *Life of Thomas Cooper*, 1872.

CROFT, LORD, *My Life of Strife*, 1948.

CUMBERLAND, RICHARD, *Memoirs*, 1807.

DARWIN, BERNARD, *The English Public School*, 1929.

DARWIN, BERNARD, *The World that Fred Made*, 1955.

DARWIN, CHARLES, *Life and Letters*, ed. by Francis Darwin, 1887.

DAVIES, G. S., *The Charterhouse in London*, 1921.

DENNIS, GEOFFREY, *Bloody Mary's*, 1934.

DUNSTERVILLE, MAJOR-GEN. L. C., *Stalky's Reminiscences*, 1928.

FINDLAY, ARTHUR, *Looking Back*, 1955.

FISHER, G. W., *Annals of Shrewsbury School*, 1899.

FLECKER, JAMES ELROY, *Some Letters from Abroad*, 1930.

FORSTER, E. M., *Goldsworthy Lowes Dickinson*, 1934.

FORSTER, JOHN, *Life of Charles Dickens*, 1871–4.

GASKELL, C. M., *Records of an Eton Schoolboy*, 1883.

GIBBON, A. M., *The Ancient Free Grammar School of Skipton*, 1947.

GILL, ERIC, *Autobiography*, 1940.

GRAHAM, J. P., *Forty Years of Uppingham*, 1932.

GRANTLEY, LORD, *Silver Spoon*, 1954.

GRAVES, A. P., *To Return to All That*, 1950.

GRAVES, CHARLES, *The Bad Old Days*, 1951.

GRAY, J. M., *History of Perse School*, 1921.

GREENE, GRAHAM, (editor), *The Old School*, 1934.

GRIER, REV. R. M., *John Allen, A Memoir*, 1889.

HAKE, T. G., *Memories of Eighty Years*, 1892.

HANDFORD, B. W. T., *History of St Mary and Nicholas College, Lancing*, 1933.

HART-DAVIS, RUPERT, *Hugh Walpole*, 1952.

HASTINGS, SIR PATRICK, *Autobiography*, 1948.

HEITLAND, W., *After Many Years*, 1925.

HENDERSON, B. L. K., *Thirty Years Hard*, 1933.

HINE, R. L., *Confessions of an Uncommon Attorney*, 1945.

HOGG, T. J., *Life of Shelley*, 1858.

HOLDER, C. S., *An Anthology of School Verse*, 1928.

HOOLE, CHARLES, *A New Discovery of the Old Art of Teaching Schoole*, 1660.

HOUSMAN, LAURENCE, *The Unexpected Years*, 1937.

HOWSON, E. W., and WARNER, G. T., *Harrow School*, 1898.

HUGHES, SPIKE, *Opening Bars*, 1946.

HUGHES, THOMAS, *Tom Brown's Schooldays*, 1857.

HUNT, LEIGH, *Autobiography*, 1850.

HUTTON, WILLIAM, *Autobiography*, 1816.

HUXLEY, T. H., *Autobiography*, 1890.

JAMESON, E. M., *Charterhouse (English Public Schools)*, 1937.

KEPPEL, GEORGE T., EARL OF ALBEMARLE, *Fifty Years of My Life*, 1876.

KINGLAKE, A. W., *Eothen*, 1844.

KIPLING, RUDYARD, *Something of Myself*, 1937.

KNOX, VICESIMUS, *Winter Evenings*, 1790.

LAMB, CHARLES, Recollections of Christ's Hospital, Christ's Hospital Five-and-Thirty Years Ago. (*Gentleman's Magazine*, 1813), *Essays of Elia*, 1823.

LAMB, G. F., *The English at School*, 1950.

LANSBURY, GEORGE, *My Life*, 1928.

LEACH, A. F., *A History of Winchester College*, 1899.

LEACH, A. F., *Schools of Medieval England*, 1915.

LOCKWOOD, EDWARD, *Early Days at Marlborough College*, 1893.

LYTE, H. C. MAXWELL, *A History of Eton College*, 1911.

MACK, E. C., *Public Schools and British Opinion*, 1938.

MACREADY, W. C., *Reminiscences*, 1875.

MAIS, S. P. B., *Buffets and Rewards*, 1952.

MALET, SIR ALEXANDER, *Some Account of the System of Fagging at Winchester School*, 1828.

MANSFIELD, R. B., *School Life at Winchester College* (1834–40), 1870.

MARROT, H. V., *Life and Letters of John Galsworthy*, 1935.

MAYO, C. H. P., *Reminiscences of a Harrow Master*, 1928.

McDONNELL, M. F. J., *A History of St Paul's School*, 1909.

MERIVALE, HERMAN, *Bar, Stage, and Platform*, 1902.

MILNE, A. A., *It's Too Late Now*, 1939.

MINCHIN, J. G. COTTON, *Old Harrow Days*, 1898.

MITFORD, M. R., *Our Village*, 1824–32.

MONCRIEFF, A. R. HOPE, *A Book About Schools*, 1925.

NEWBOLT, SIR F. G., *Clifton College Forty Years Ago*, 1927.

NORWOOD, SIR CYRIL, *The English Tradition in Education*, 1929.

'O.E.', *Eton Under Hornby*, 1910.

OGILVIE, VIVIAN, *The English Public School*, 1957.

OLD ETONIAN, *A Letter to Sir Alexander Malet*, 1828.

PALMER, ROUNDELL, EARL OF SELBORNE, *Memorials*, 1896.

PASCOE, C. E., *Everyday Life in Our Public Schools*, 1881.

PEACHAM, HENRY, *The Compleat Gentleman*, 1622.

PEARCE, JESSE, Article in *Chambers's Journal*, March 1951.

PITCAIRN, E. H., *Unwritten Laws*, 1899.

PRINGLE, PATRICK, *When They Were Boys*, 1954.

PROTHERO, R. E., *Life and Letters of Dean Stanley*, 1894.

QUICK, R. H., *Essays on Educational Reformers*, 1868.

ROBERTSON-GLASGOW, R. C., *46 Not Out*, 1948.

RODGERS, JOHN, *The Old Public Schools of England*, 1938.

ROE, W. N. (editor), *Public Schools Cricket*, 1951.

ROUSE, W. H. D., *A History of Rugby School*, 1898.

SELINCOURT, AUBREY DE, *The Schoolmaster*, 1951.

SHORE, W. TEIGNMOUTH, *Westminster School*, 1910.

SITWELL, SIR OSBERT, *The Scarlet Tree*, 1950.

SMITH, REV. SYDNEY, Essays in *Edinburgh Review*, August 1810, October 1809.

SNELL, F. J., *Blundell's*, 1928.

SOMERVELL, D. C., *A History of Tonbridge School*, 1947.

SOUTHEY, ROBERT, *Recollections of Early Life*, 1820-21.

STAFFORD, H., *A History of Caterham School*, 1945.

STANLEY, A. P., *Life and Correspondence of Thomas Arnold*, 1845.

STAUNTON, HOWARD, *The Great Schools of England*, 1865.

STEPHENS, W. R. W., *Life and Letters of Dean Hook*, 1879.

STRACHEY, LYTTON, *Eminent Victorians*, 1918.

TANNER, L. E., *Westminster School*, 1934.

THOMPSON, D'ARCY, *Day-dreams of a Schoolmaster*, 1864.

THOMPSON, D'ARCY, *Wayside Thoughts*, 1868.

Times, The, March 1825, April 1854, July 1877.

Times Educational Supplement, The, December 1957, January 1958.

THOMSON, SIR BASIL, *The Scene Changes*, 1939.

TREDCROFT, C. L., *Recollections of Seventy Years*, 1904.

TRENCH, REV. FRANCIS, *A Few Notes from Past Life* (1818–32), 1862.

TROLLOPE, ANTHONY, *An Autobiography*, 1883.

TROLLOPE, T. A., *What I Remember*, 1887.

TUCKWELL, REV. W., *The Ancient Ways*, 1893.

TUPPER, MARTIN, *My Life as an Author*, 1886.

WAKEFIELD, GILBERT, *Memoirs*, 1792.

WALLACE, ALFRED RUSSELL, *My Life*, 1905.

WALPOLE, HUGH, *The Crystal Box*, 1924.

WALPOLE, SPENCER, *Life of Lord John Russell*, 1889.

WARWICK AND BROOKE, EARL OF, *Memories of Sixty Years*, 1917.

WATSON, FOSTER, *The Old Grammar Schools*, 1916.

WAUGH, ALEC, *Public School Life*, 1922.

WEST, J. M., *Shrewsbury (English Public Schools)*, 1937.

WHITEHOUSE, J. H. (editor), *The English Public School*, 1919.

WILKINS, H. T., *Great English Schools*, 1925.

WILKINSON, REV. C. A., *Reminiscences of Eton*, 1888.

WILLIAMSON, H. R., *The Ancient Capital (Winchester)*, 1953.

WILSON, J. DOVER (editor), *Life in Shakespeare's England*, 1911.

WYMER, NORMAN, *Dr Arnold of Rugby*, 1953.

INDEX